Be Still ~ Bear Fruit offers an effective way to reconnect with God and others with a deeper sense of self. It shows how contemplation can enrich our every day lives, whatever our beliefs may be. It is biblically centered, theologically sound, profound yet very clear, practical, and inspirational. With insight, beauty, and wisdom, stories of both Christian and non-Christian traditions, Rev. Andrews shows that the means to spiritual well being are within us all. When you have read and lived this book, you have been in touch with the best that world spirituality has to offer. It is ideal for both the individual reader and study groups.

—*Rev. George Alengadan Ph.D.*
Adjunct Professor, Graduate Theological Union,
Berkeley, California

Doing nothing, being everything, and enjoying the fullness of life in God are challenges to our present modern day culture that is not only restless, but also has no time for life in the Spirit. *Be Still ~ Bear Fruit* summons us to drop the habit of "getting our prayers in" and take the risk of plunging into deep silence, to be with the indwelling presence of God. It is only this experience that has the power to bring about the change that we wish to see in others and ourselves. It is indeed a spiritual treat.

—*Loretta Anjali, India*

Be Still ~ Bear Fruit invites us to take a step back from our fast-paced life and spirituality and enter into a deeper and true spiritual experience of God. Words cannot explain the beauty of such an experience of God. The book invites us to go beyond words and to take a spiritual leap into a deeper prayer life, thereby, to a closer loving, living union, and intimacy with God. It is centered in Christ, but at the same time it is universal. It will surely appeal to all who are searching for an intimate experience of God.

—*Dr. Cindy Walton D.P.T., Fremont, CA*

Intimacy with God is elusive. *Be Still ~ Bear Fruit* points the way to develop a deep and lasting relationship with God with its' in depth exploration of prayer, meditation, spiritual discipline, forgiveness, nonviolence, sharing, gratitude, and other themes. This book deserves a slow read with time set for meditating on the themes present. The practical aids and scripture references help not only to develop each topic but also challenge the reader to *Live Our True Nature.*

—*Sr. Patricia Burke, SMSM Boston*

Be Still ~ Bear Fruit presents Christocentric contemplation in a wonderful and meaningful way as a call to all. It presents Jesus Christ as the summit of all human endeavors and experiences. Though it is Christocentric, still it is universal in nature, it reaches out and will appeal to everyone. The various themes reflected therein call for a personal response. The book bears rereading and revisiting. We found its messages timely and (unfortunately) consistently timely.

—*John and Laurie Kennedy, San Leandro, CA.*

After I finished reading *Be Still ~ Bear Fruit* I said to my husband, "I feel like I just finished having a wonderful meal. I feel spiritually filled." The book is a must for all those who are searching for depth in prayer life. Silence and stillness in prayer bring us to an experience of God and it is this experience that transforms our life. It is a book for all, even for those who are caught in the business of life's daily challenges. The *"practical guide,"* the *"amusing anecdotes,"* and *"prayer"* at the end of each chapter make it excellent spiritual reading.

—*Linda O. Roura, JMJ Mission, Philippines*

BE STILL ~ BEAR FRUIT

Living Our True Nature

Andrews Amritharaj, Ph.D.

Book Design and Printing by Falcon Books

San Ramon, California

ISBN 10: 0-9778860-0-X
ISBN 13: 978-0-9778860-0-5

Published by
Sadhaana Publication

e-mail: bstill2know@yahoo.com

All biblical references are taken from The Revised
Standard Version of the Holy Bible (Catholic Edition).

The statistics given in the chapter on Sharing were taken
from: "When Did I See You Hungry?"
a film by Gerard Thomas Straub, it is available from
www.SanDamiano Foundation.org

PRINTED IN THE UNITED STATES OF AMERICA

Dedicated to my dear parents who lovingly sowed in me
the first seeds of faith and taught me how to pray.

Henry + Marty:

God's love is
more real than
our every shadows

Fr. Andrews.

Acknowledgement

This book would not have come to fruition without the assistance and cooperation of many who have helped me. My profound and heartfelt gratitude:

- to my parents and my brothers and sisters who have always supported and encouraged me in my journey of faith.
- to Anjali, Sandhya, and Sanjay for always being there for me and to Rev. Jerome Vallabaraj, S.D.B. who has remained a very good friend to me. Their friendship and support have been a source of blessing and strength for me to finish this book.
- to Rev. Gerald Brown, S.S., Ph.D., for writing the foreword introducing this book. I have been inspired by his spirit of optimism, his realistic attitude to life, and his love and openness to and for multi-culturalism.
- to Rev. Wayne Campbell, who encouraged me to write articles in "Andy's Corner," the weekly parish bulletin, in which the first seeds of this book were planted.
- to the parishioners of St. Felicitas Catholic Church in San Leandro; they not only were a receptive congregation, listening to my homilies, of which most of my thoughts have been expressed herein, but their comments have encouraged me to "put into writing" what I had shared with them.

- to Rev. Dominic Thuong for providing the quiet space that I needed to finish this project and also to Rev. William Rosario for his constant encouragement and genuine friendship.
- to Sandi Walton, Monica Haupt, Sheila Bickerton, Michael and Julie Apel, Ken and Theresa Schexnayder, and Mary Lou Ramirez who in various and different ways have helped and assisted me in this project and for their interest in reading the manuscript and making necessary suggestions and changes that have helped me to improve the structure and content of this book.
- to Robert Jost for generously sharing the photograph taken by him that marks the front cover of this book and to Kurt Burton Photography for the photo on the back cover.
- to the many friends who have continually shown a keen interest, encouragement, and unflagging enthusiasm that have inspired me to complete this book.

May God bless them and their families!

Contents

Foreword

It was a great honor for me to be asked by Father Andrews Amritharaj, my friend and colleague, to write this foreword. He is a man of extraordinary experience and talent. An Indian and Catholic Christian by birth who lived side by side and in friendship with men and women of other religious traditions, he knows how to bridge the contributions of the East and the West to human and spiritual development. He knows both how to learn and to teach, to receive and to give. As a Salesian priest, he embraces religious life from the inside out and at the same time desires to know as fully as possible the hungers and thirsts of today's fellow human beings, including the most simple and ordinary among us. As a moral theologian, he is sensitive both to the ethical principles and practices of leading a virtuous life and, at the same time, to the all-important role of stillness, quiet, and contemplative prayer in helping us to realize our destiny as men and women totally caught up in the love of God for all creation and us. As one who helps to train diocesan priests for spiritual leadership in the Church and as a parish priest himself, he knows the challenge of becoming increasingly human and holy. Most importantly, he is a warm, compassionate, loving man who reverences the other and who desires that all of us connect more intimately with our God and with all of our brothers and sisters in God.

The title of the book is highly instructive: **Be Still ~ Bear Fruit: Living our True Nature.** In my experience, one of the greatest struggles for most of us in today's contemporary culture is coming to know and experience the presence of God in our lives. To do this, we need to be truly still, quiet, present to God. The truth is that God is already present to us. Our problem is that often we are too busy, running in too many directions to notice, to be sufficiently aware, and to make the necessary connections. Meister Eckhart once said wisely: "The very best and utmost act of attainment in this life is to remain still and let God act and speak in thee." Only when we experience communion with God in quiet and in prayer can we truly live the gifts of the Spirit in word and in deed. Only then can we bear fruit. And bear fruit we must! It is indeed in becoming still and in living authentically that we come to know and live our true nature. How to do all this more freely and with joy is what **Be Still ~ Bear Fruit** hopes to teach all of us.

I was inspired when Father Andrews told me that he wants this book to be intelligible and meaningful to his mom and others like her. I can assure him that his book will realize his dreams. His mom will love the book as I have loved it. It is a book that will help all of us Christians come to deeper insight into the nature of human life itself, to the gift of Jesus Christ in our lives, and to the multiple ways God addresses the human heart. It can also be instructive and helpful for our brothers and sisters of other religious traditions, especially those coming from the East. Father Andrews drew heavily from their experience and writings in ways I found to be enlightening and immensely helpful.

Surely, the reverse can be equally true. Father Andrews, we are all grateful for your gift of self to all of us! We pray for the gift of stillness, union with God, and service to our brothers and sisters throughout the world.

—*Rev. Gerald Brown, S.S., Ph.D.*
President
St. Patrick's Seminary and University
Menlo Park, CA

Introduction

Be Still ~ Bear Fruit: Living Our True Nature has evolved as an attempt to understand the biblical call to be still and know God. It deals with the meaning of stillness, silence, solitude, experience of God, true self, and self that bears fruit in our everyday life.

The first four chapters constitute the first part of the book: *Be Still.* The different chapters are not independent units, but interrelated, each one leading to the other. The first chapter considers prayer without words; it highlights the understanding that in stillness and silence, it is truly possible to experience union, intimacy, and oneness with God. Prayer, in such an experience, in the words of St. Teresa of Avila, "is to be in the presence of God who loves us." The theme in the second chapter, flowing from the first, presents the truth that in the presence of God we realize the true nature of the self. Chapters three and four continue with the theme of self-realization in the presence of God, by constantly walking on the spiritual path of meditation (the emphasis here is not on any particular type or technique of meditation, but on the "why" and on the importance of meditation) that calls for a life of spiritual discipline.

Experience of unitive consciousness, beyond all forms of dualities in stillness and silence, is a return to the center, to our true nature. Unitive consciousness is the true nature of the self, and the fruit of the Spirit constitutes the true nature of the self. Thus, it is not that we consciously choose to forgive, but the very nature of the self is forgiveness; not that we choose to perform acts of nonviolence, but the self is nonviolent; not that we choose to do acts of compassion, but the core of the self is compassion.

Jesus says, "... He who abides in me, and I in him, he it is that bears much fruit, ..." (Jn 15:5). Experiencing God in stillness and silence and remaining with and in God, bears fruit in our life. Spiritual life is not only an experience of unitive consciousness and being still, but allowing the experience of stillness to flow into our daily life. The self will begin to bear fruit only when the self that realizes itself in stillness and silence is the same self that manifests itself in our mental, vocal, and physical acts. Self flows from the center toward the circumference. Our actions are an extension of who we are, the very core of our being. In the remaining chapters, which form the second part of this book, *Bear Fruit,* I chose to reflect on some of the fruit of the self: forgiveness, nonviolence, sharing, gratitude, and towards an understanding of evil, suffering, pain, and jealousy.

Thus, stillness before and in God is not a negative and empty stillness. It is not a stillness that is content to look at itself, but rather it is a stillness that is opened to the presence of God within us. In stillness, in the presence of God, self-realization is made possible. It is a stillness that brings us to our very own center, to an experience and realization of our true self. It is a stillness that is complete. It is a stillness that will enable us to bear fruit in our life.

Be Still ~ Bear Fruit essentially revolves around the person of Jesus Christ, as he is the model par excellence of how to be still and know God. In Jesus we encounter a person, who not only experienced his heavenly Father in stillness, but also one in whom his words and actions were an expression and extension of his experience of his heavenly Father. Jesus is not only for admiration, but a living presence to be imitated. Hence, most of the chapters constantly return to the person of Jesus, his ministry, and his teachings. In understanding Jesus and his teachings we will fully understand our own call to be still and know God.

Being born and raised in a predominantly non-Christian culture, I have also had the opportunity of being exposed to and influenced by the understanding of stillness and silence from non-Christian sources. I realize that such influences have been positive and also enriching in my understanding of stillness bearing fruit. Although, my focus in this book is primarily Christian, non-Christian resources are evident in the development of certain themes contained herein.

My prayer is that living in this "fast-paced" culture we will discover within these pages reflections that can help us to be still and know God and to find true peace, joy, and fulfillment by living your true nature.

—*Andrews Amritharaj*
Menlo Park
Easter 2006

Prayer: To Be in the Presence of God

Prayer is to be with the one who loves us.
—St. Teresa of Avila

We pray best when we don't even know we are praying.
—St. Anthony of the Desert

Experiential and Acquired Knowledge

A friend met Mulla Nasrudin and his newly born baby in the market place. His friend remarked to Nasrudin, "God has blessed you with a beautiful child!" Nasrudin replied, "You should see his photographs."

Human beings tend to be more satisfied and contented with appearances than reality itself. Once I accompanied a friend to St. Peter's Basilica in Rome. While I was explaining to him the history, art, and architecture, he was busy taking photographs. I said to him, "You have come a long way to see this famous basilica. Look at it, appreciate the art, the beauty, and feel the history." He replied, "The Basilica is so beautiful. I will take pictures of it and see it at home." Pictures of the Basilica can be purchased from the streets of Rome, but the purpose, the direct contact, and the immediate experience of what he came for was lost. We are losing touch with reality, and the irony of it is that we not only think and accept appearance as real, but we also seem to be comfortable with it as well.

There are different kinds of knowledge. Knowledge can be acquired by reading books or listening to discourses, speeches, homilies, attending conferences, and by participating in seminars. Knowledge, gained both by reading and listening to others, surmounts information, insights, interpretations, collected wisdom, and experiences of various speakers and authors. Such knowledge can either be religious, philosophical, theological, scientific, empirical, practical, rational, or academic. We depend on others for these different types of knowledge. For example, my knowledge of geology is solely based on the research of geologists. This knowledge is both informational and intellectual. The second type of knowledge is the result of my own experience, my direct contact with reality itself. It is experiential, immediate, and personal. For example, a person who has not had an experiential contact with snow will only understand the meaning of the word "snow" by association of various concepts and through the process of comparison, but for someone who has had direct contact with snow, the word "snow" will acquire a completely different meaning. Similarly, for a person who has never visited the Taj Mahal, it is just a monument, but for those who have personally been to the Taj Mahal, the very mention of its name will evoke altogether a different kind of meaning. Acquired knowledge is necessary and has certain advantages, but experiential knowledge is not only direct and immediate, it is also an experience of truth in itself.

G.N. Goenka, a *vipassana* teacher, shares the following story during *vipassana* retreats. There were two young boys, one of who was blind from birth; they lived by begging and at night they slept inside the temple. One day the blind boy stayed back in the temple because he was ill and his friend went to the village to collect food for both of them. When he came back he told his friend, "Today a family gave me some delicious milk pudding, but I am sorry I could not bring you some as I did not have a proper container." The blind boy asked his friend, "Tell me, what is milk pudding?" His friend replied, "It is white and sweet." His friend, blind from birth, did not understand the meaning of the word, "white" so then asked him, "Tell me what is white?" "White is opposite of black," explained his friend. "What is black?" asked the blind boy. His friend looked around and saw a white crane, caught it and holding the bird in front of his friend said, "White is like this bird." The blind boy touched the bird and said, "Now I understand that white is soft and fluffy." His friend said, "Oh no, white is white. Try to understand." The blind boy once again examined the bird moving his hand from the beak to the tip of the tail, turned to his friend and said, "Now I understand that white is not only soft and fluffy, but also crooked."

No matter how hard he tried to explain the meaning of white to his blind friend, his friend could not grasp the direct, immediate, and experiential meaning of white as his own understanding of white had always been mediated by various other concepts.

Knowledge of God

Is our knowledge of God acquired and mediated or experiential and personal? If our knowledge of God begins as an acquired knowledge and as this knowledge of God deepens, do we make the necessary transition from an acquired knowledge to a more personal and experiential knowledge of God? To the question, "Why did God make you?" The Baltimore Catholic Catechism answer is, "To know, to love, and to serve God." How do we know God? What type of knowledge is necessary in order to love and serve God? How do we acquire knowledge of God? Catechism, philosophy, theology, religious books, and spiritual discourses are all great resources for acquiring wonderful concepts, ideas, and categories about God and can even arouse a burning desire to know and love God, but will concepts, ideas, and categories alone enable us to realize and live the biblical call to "know God?" In the Bible "know God" is an intimate, personal, involved, experiential, and committed knowledge, a knowledge that elicits a personal response to enter into love and communion with God. How and from where does our knowledge of God begin?

When we were children, our parents and religion teachers initiated us into religion and religious practices, and we learned to relate to God by using words, images, symbols, and rituals. At this age, religion mostly operated on the level of "shoulds" and "ought tos" using reward, approval, punishment, and guilt as powerful tools. As we become adults the introjected religious values, duties, commands, and obligations from outside should be personalized and internalized. As our spiritual life deepens, the need, the desire to pray and to worship, and to enter into a living relationship with God should arise out of our own "felt need of God" and not out of obligation or obedience to a religious superego. Eventually, acquired knowledge of God, should give way to an experiential knowledge of God. In the words of St. John of the Cross, it is the "night of sense," a spiritual growing up, a transition into a mature relationship with God, a transition from an acquired knowledge to an experiential and personal knowledge of God.

For many, the time-tested spiritual and religious practices of the Christian tradition seem to satisfy the spiritual longings of the human heart; but the most important question is, do we really allow these spiritual practices to lead us to an experience of God, or do they stop at the level of mental consciousness? In my prayer life do I long for and strive to experience the oneness with God that Jesus often speaks about in the gospel of John? Is my prayer really an experience of God, or is it just a repetition of words, or is it only a prayer of petition? After the multiplication of the loaves, when people were looking for Jesus, he said to them, "Truly, truly, I say to you, you seek me, not because you saw signs, but because you ate your fill of the loaves. Do not labor for the food which perishes, but for the food which endures to eternal life, which the Son of man will give to you; for on him has God the Father set his seal" (Jn 6:26-27). What am I really seeking in my prayer life? Is it just to fulfill a religious obligation, or is it only a mere repetition of words said in a hurry, or is it an effort to seek just the loaves of this world, or is it life with God, a life of union and intimacy with God?

Prayer Without Words

Vocal prayers, mental prayers, popular devotions, novenas, celebration of sacramentals and rituals were part of our spirituality as we grew, and they did have tremendous meaning as faith became part of our life. There was also the danger of reducing spirituality and our relationship with God "to getting our prayers in" regularly and performing certain religious devotions and practices as attempts to please God. To pray only with words, literally reading/saying our prayers, is to limit and deprive ourselves of the beauty and the possibility of entering deeply into divine union and intimacy with God. To continue to be at the level of vocal and mental prayer is to remain at the surface level of spiritual life; it is to refuse to plunge into deeper layers of union and intimacy with God.

Words, however deeply spiritual and theological they may be, can only point to the invincible mystery. Words, at most, can only bring us to the threshold of God, who can never be fully captured, contained, or understood in human words. St. Augustine said, "If you understand it, it isn't God." Every addition to God is a subtraction. Dionysius the Areopagite was known for his process of unknowing. Thomas Aquinas used the *via negativa* in talking about God. He said that the only thing we can say about God is that God is not what God is, and towards the end of his life after a direct experience of God, he considered everything he had written as straw compared to the experience of God. For Moses Maimmondes, God can only be described in negative terms. The classical Hinduism taught the *neti, neti* (not this, not this) method of knowing God. Every affirmation of God is, in a way, a negation of what God is. To be still and silent in the presence of God is to become aware of our incapacity to capture the invincible mystery that can never be fully grasped. In order to totally experience God, we need to drop all words, human speech, and the discursive mind, and be willing to go beyond the normal, mental consciousness to be at the level of unitive consciousness that is beyond all dualities. At this level, consciousness transcends words, visuals, our imagination, and strives for conscious unity with the Absolute. It is a pure awareness of nothing but God alone.

To experience oneness, intimacy, and union with God, we have to move from praying with words to a prayer without words. Words bring us to the realm of the relationship with God, but words cannot substitute the relationship itself. Doesn't Jesus himself say in the gospel, "You search the scriptures, because you think that in them you have eternal life; and it is they that bear witness to me; yet you refuse to come to me that you may have life" (Jn 5:39)? What is the use of holding onto that which is pointing to the reality and refusing to hold the reality itself?

Gautama Buddha used to say, "When I point to the moon, look at the moon and not at my finger that is pointing to the moon." The role of the finger is just to point to the moon and nothing more. What is the use of holding onto the finger and refusing to behold the moon? He also uses another metaphor. "When you have crossed the river, leave the raft behind. Do not carry the raft into town because it has helped you cross the river." The function of the raft is to help someone to cross the river and with that its function comes to an end. The purpose of the words, however wonderful they are, is to point the way and to lead us to the threshold of the invincible mystery that can only be experienced beyond words, in stillness and silence. Words have a certain purpose and beyond that function we should have the courage to drop the words and enter into that sublime silence of body and mind, to be present to God alone.

A famous philosopher stopped by a cobbler's shop to have his shoes repaired. Upon completion of the job, as he was leaving, he said to the cobbler, "Are you feeling bad to hold in your hands the shoes and the sandals that are constantly exposed to dirt, filth, and dust of the roads?" The cobbler calmly replied, "Sir, tell me are you feeling bad to hold in your mind the words and ideas of others?" Often our knowledge of God, however deep and noble it may be is the experience and the words of others. Others can share with us their spiritual journeys and stories. Their stories and writings can inspire us, motivate us, and point the way for us. Even prayers written by saints are beautiful, but they are still their experiences of God. Are we only repeating their experiences when we pray their prayers, or do we allow them to lead us to our own experience of God? St. Paul writing to the community at Corinth says:

> But we impart a secret and hidden wisdom of God, which God decreed before the ages for our glorification... But, as it is written, 'What no eye has seen, nor ear heard, nor the heart of man conceived, what God has prepared for those who love him,' God has revealed to us through the Spirit. For the Spirit searches everything, even the depths of God" (1 Cor 2:7, 9-10).

In prayer without words, we are with the one whom the eyes cannot see or the ears cannot hear; we are just present to, and are with, this hidden mystery. "As a hart longs for flowing streams, ..." (Ps 42:1) and "... more than the watchmen for the morning, ..." (Ps 130:6), so too, our soul longs for God. Prayer, beyond words and in silence, is satiating this thirst and longing for the experience of intimacy and union with God.

In the beginning, when two people fall in love, words play an important part in the building up of the relationship between the two. Love, mutual admiration, and appreciation are expressed in words. As love grows deeper and deeper, the lovers transcend their need for words and just remain in and with each other. At this stage, the need for words is minimal and at a deeper level in their presence to each other, words are completely dropped and they find fulfillment and happiness in just being with the other. They are just present to each other in silence. This silence is beautiful; it is not an empty silence, but a silence filled with the presence of each other. Lovers, at times, say nothing to each other, but are present to each other just by holding each others' hand. Isn't it a common human experience that the deepest human emotions are expressed not so much with words, but in a comforting hug and in just being with the other person? Words that were essential at the beginning of the relationship are dropped at the height of the relationship. Words that are spoken now proceed from the depth of their love for each other, and the words take on a completely new meaning, filled with genuine and true love. It is their presence to one another that gives meaning to their words. Something similar also happens in prayer without words. In the beginning words are used to address our need and desire for God and to enter into a relationship with God. Words take us to the threshold of the relationship with God. Once we have entered into this loving relationship with God, words are not necessary any longer and they should be dropped. It is this intimacy and relationship with God that finds its expression in mental, vocal prayer, and in the celebration of rituals.

Jesus' Prayer in Solitude

A disciple allows himself to be guided by the master and through a life of discipline; following the teachings and the example of the master, the disciple tries to become like the master himself. Jesus is our Lord, teacher, and master, and we are his disciples. As his disciples, Jesus invites us to follow him, "Come, follow me!" This invitation to follow Jesus is not only to follow him in his public ministry, but also to follow him in his prayer life, which was the source and foundation of his public ministry. Through a life of spiritual discipline, we allow ourselves to be guided and fashioned by the prayer life of Jesus, and through a consistent spiritual practice we try to experience what Jesus experienced in his own prayer life.

What was prayer for Jesus? We would say prayer for Jesus was talking to God, listening to God, having a dialogue, an act of adoration, giving thanks, worship, praise, and glory to God, discerning his Father's will, and interceding with God on our behalf. All these are true. More than all of these, prayer for Jesus was to be with the one who loved him and to be in the presence of his heavenly Father. In the Trinity, Jesus as the Son relates to his Father, and the flow of love between the Father and the Son is the Spirit. The Holy Trinity is a wonderful model of three persons in love and in communion with each other. In the Trinity it is their relationship and love for each other that enables them to realize their identities, and yet at the same time maintain their individual nature as Father, Son, and Spirit. Love is the basis of their communion with each other. When he was on this earth, Jesus longed for this love and union with his heavenly Father. Jesus was passionately in love with his heavenly Father. It was a love that could not be satisfied by anything in this world except by the presence of his heavenly Father. Prayer for Jesus was seeking out the presence, intimacy, and the experience of his heavenly Father.

Jesus' entire life was a prayer, a life of intimacy with God and a life of living in the presence of God. This intimacy and experience of God was lived out both in his prayer in solitude and his communal prayer. Jesus, as a pious Jew, participated in the prayers at Synagogue. He went to the synagogue with his disciples. He read and interpreted the Scriptures. This is Jesus joining the common prayer of his people. Besides the communal prayer, the gospels also portray a Jesus who prayed in solitude:

> And when you pray, you must not be like the hypocrites; for they love to stand and pray in the synagogues and at the street corners, that they may be seen by men. Truly, I say to you, they have their reward. But when you pray, go into your room and shut the door and pray to your Father who is in secret; and your Father who sees in secret will reward you. And in praying do not heap up empty phrases as the Gentiles do; for they think that they will be heard for their many words. Do not be like them, for your Father knows what you need before you ask him (Mt 6:5-8).

In the above passage the emphasis is on the need to pray in solitude, in private. Privacy is not just external but also internal. While praying, Jesus tells us not to use too many words, that there is a prayer deeper than the prayer of petition because, "... your Father knows what you need before you ask him" (Mt 6:8).

In the gospels it seems to appear that more importance is given to Jesus' prayer in solitude than to his communal prayer:

> ➤ And in the morning, a great while before day, he rose and went out to a lonely place, and there he prayed (Mk 1:35).
> ➤ And after he had taken leave of them, he went into the hills to pray (Mk 6:46).
> ➤ In these days he went out into the hills to pray; and all night he continued in prayer to God (Lk 6:12).
> ➤ But so much the more the report went abroad concerning him; and great multitudes gathered to hear and to be healed of their infirmities. But he withdrew to the wilderness and prayed (Lk 5:15-16).
> ➤ Now when all the people were baptized, and when Jesus also had been baptized and was praying, the heaven was opened, and the Holy Spirit descended upon him in bodily form, as a dove, and a voice came from heaven, "Thou art my beloved Son; with thee I am well pleased" (Lk 3: 21-22).
> ➤ Now about eight days after these sayings he took with him Peter and John and James, and went up on the mountain to pray (Lk 9:28).
> ➤ Now it happened that as he was praying alone the disciples were with him; and he asked them, "Who do the people say that I am?" (Lk 9:18).
> ➤ He was praying in a certain place, and when he ceased, one of his disciples said to him,

"Lord, teach us to pray, as John taught his disciples" (Lk 11:1).

The above biblical references present a Jesus who longed for prayer in solitude. I often wonder how it was possible for him to pray late into the nights and then again, as the gospels portray, he was in prayer long before sunrise. After traversing the dusty roads of Palestine on foot, preaching, healing people, and confronting the Scribes and the Pharisees, Jesus must have been very tired. In spite of his fatigue, he still longed for prayer in solitude. For Jesus, time spent in solitude was so special and close to his heart that he chose mountains, deserts and times during which he did not want to be disturbed by others. It appears as though Jesus would not have compromised this time for anything else. Why? Because the time he spent exclusively with God was a time of deep inner experience, union, intimacy, and oneness with his Father. It was an experience that not only rejuvenated his tired body and mind, filling him with energy and strength, but also an experience that was the center and focus of his entire life. It was indeed his "daily bread."

Prayer as an Experience of Oneness with God

Jesus taught his disciples the "Our Father," but the gospels do not tell us how Jesus prayed during those moments in solitude. What is certain is that he prayed and cherished his prayer in solitude. From other references in the gospels, we can infer the effect of this prayer on Jesus. Luke 11:1 depicts Jesus in prayer. One of the disciples must have seen the effect of prayer, the radiance that shone on the face of Jesus as the result of his communion with his heavenly Father, that he asked him to teach them to pray. Again, in the Transfiguration scene Luke says, "And as he was praying, the appearance of his countenance was altered, and his raiment became dazzling white" (Lk 9:29). The effect that prayer had on Jesus was the result of what John constantly refers to: Jesus' experience of oneness, union, intimacy, and communion with his heavenly Father. Prayer, for Jesus, was being present to and being with the Father:

> ➤ Jesus often spoke of the experience of his oneness with his Father: "Do you not believe that I am in the Father and the Father in me? The words that I say to you I do not speak on my own authority; but the Father who dwells in me does his works. Believe me that I am in the Father and the Father in me; or else believe me for the sake of the works themselves" (Jn 14:10-11). "... that they may all be one; even as thou, Father, art in me, and I in thee..." (Jn 17:21).
> ➤ To experience oneness with God is to experience oneness with others: "In that day you will know that I am in my Father, and you in me, and I in you" (Jn 14:20).
> ➤ Prayer is indwelling love, love opening itself to Love: "Jesus answered him, "If a man loves me, he will keep my word, and my Father will

love him, and we will come to him and make our home with him" (Jn 14:23).

➤ As Jesus, who was with his Father, we as God's children also were in God experiencing oneness with God even before we were born into this world. Prayer without words is a longing for the oneness with God even while we are living here on earth. It is an experience of the unitive consciousness with and in God: "I came from the Father and have come into the world; again, I am leaving the world and going to the Father" (Jn 16:28). "... and now, Father, glorify thou me in thy own presence with the glory which I had with thee before the world was made" (Jn 17:5).

➤ In John 17, Jesus often tells his disciples that he came from his Father and was returning to his Father and during the time that he was on this earth he knew that he was always with and living in his Father. He experienced this oneness, and that's what he prayed for his disciples: "... that they may be one, even as we are one" (Jn 17:11). Again in verse 23 he prays: "I in them and thou in me, that they may become perfectly one, ..." and in verse 26 he comes back to this theme, "I made known to them thy name, and I will make it known, that the love with which thou hast loved me may be in them, and I in them."

Prayer in solitude, for Jesus, were moments of experiences of oneness, intimacy, and union with his Father. For Jesus prayer in solitude were not moments of vocal and mental prayers, but a direct and immediate experience of God. Jesus, who experienced oneness, intimacy, and union with his Father in the transcendent Trinity, continued to experience this intimacy and union even as Jesus of Nazareth. Jesus prayed that we too, experience this divine intimacy and union with our Father in heaven, not only in the life to come, but also in our life here on this earth. Before we were born into this world, we were with God, living in God, united to God, experiencing a unitive consciousness in and with God. Even during our life here on earth, the heart longs for such union and intimacy with God. This is possible when the mind transcends all forms of duality and division and, in silence and stillness, becomes present to God alone.

Prayer is to be with the one who loves us. The emphasis is on *to be*. It is being still both in mind and body, just *being*. True love, at its depth, transcends all necessity for words. It is our loving presence that really matters, and prayer without words is the deepest loving presence to God, a presence that is always accompanied by God's gift of grace and light. It is a presence that culminates in the experience of oneness with God. Why should we be satisfied with mere words and intellectual knowledge of God when the deepest experience of God is possible?

When we go beyond words, images, and the discursive mind, we are able to enter into the depth of our very own being, where the indwelling presence of God is always present. Prayer is to become aware of and realize the indwelling presence of God within us.

The Book of Revelation affirms this truth: "Behold, I stand at the door and knock; if any one hears my voice and opens the door, I will come in to him and eat with him, and he with me" (Rev 3:20). In prayer without words, we drop the many doors of illusions that prevent us from beholding the presence of God in us. In this prayer the wandering mind is brought under control, and both the body and the mind in stillness and silence remains before and in the presence of God. Through prayer without words we are able to enter into silence, to look inward and to gaze only upon God. If we believe that we have been created in the image and likeness of God, then the core of our existence is the very presence of God: "... In him we live and move and have our being" (Acts 17:28). Through this prayer we try to become aware of that deepest, unfathomable center in us where God, as the ground of existence, is always present. Becoming aware and being with that center itself is prayer. More than the act of praying, we actually become the very prayer itself. "We pray best when we don't even know we are praying" (St. Anthony of the Desert). St. Augustine said, "My heart is restless until it rests in Thee oh God." Prayer is to let the heart, mind, body, and soul be at rest in God.

Important Dimensions of Prayer Without Words

What do we need to do to experience intimacy and union with God? What are the factors that we need to cultivate for this prayer to happen? The important dimensions of prayer without words are: love for silence and solitude, primacy of experience over discursive analysis, it is Christocentric, understanding the meaning of the true self, and the efficacy of this prayer is seen by its fruit.

Silence

It is true that we can relate to God through words, rituals, symbols, images, visualization, etc., but only in silence when we are fully present to the indwelling presence of God deep within us, does our relationship with God become experiential and personal. In silence, God is not known at the intellectual level, but God is experienced. The Bible states: "Be still, and know that I am God" (Ps 46:10). It is only in silence and stillness that we truly become aware of God. Prophet Elijah finds God not in the heavy wind, nor in the loud earthquake, neither in the burning fire, but in the still small voice:

> And he said, "Go forth, and stand upon the mount before the LORD." And behold, the LORD passed by, and a great and strong wind rent the mountains, and broke in pieces the rocks before the LORD, but the LORD was not in the wind; and after the wind an earthquake, but the LORD was not in the earthquake; and after the earthquake a fire, but the LORD was not in the fire; and after the fire a still small voice. And when Elijah heard it, he wrapped his face in his mantle and went out and stood at the entrance of the cave (1Kings 19:11-13).

For prayer without words, silence is essential and in fact a must, but it is really difficult to observe and remain in silence. Three monks had decided to observe a day of silence, but after sometime one of the monks said, "Today, I shall not speak at all." The second monk said, "You have already broken the rule of silence." The third monk said, "I am the only one who has not spoken so far." How difficult it is to observe silence! In this hi-tech noise-polluted culture where speed and noise are valued and worshipped, the need for silence is rarely appreciated. In our social milieu it appears to be awkward to remain silent for a period of time. Silence is mistakenly seen as if something is wrong with the situation and it needs to be fixed. We do everything to avoid the embarrassing situation of silence. As soon as we get into our vehicles, even before we adjust the seat belt, we turn on the radio or the stereo to avoid silence. Some people feel a need to have the T.V. or radio turned on when they are home alone, just to avoid the quietness. At socials, there is so much noise that we can hardly hear each other and the more noise, the better the situation. Silence can really be frightening. We choose to avoid silence because silence leads to an inward journey that reveals our fears, insecurities, false egos, and it forces us to confront our true self.

It is indeed very difficult to be silent. The mind is like a monkey always moving, jumping, and hopping from one branch to another, and we can imagine the situation of the monkey if it is drunk. It is said that everyday there are approximately 60,000 thoughts that pass through the mind. Even during prayer, when the mind is focused on God, the mind wanders elsewhere.

In this regard Swami Sukhabodhananda shares an interesting story. A woman was chanting her prayers. As she was chanting, she remembered the milk in the oven and so, she shouts to her daughter, "Turn off the oven and make sure the milk doesn't overflow." She goes back to her chanting, and after sometime in a loud voice, she tells her son who is in the adjacent room, "Before you leave your room, make sure you turn off the fan." She returns to her chanting, and as she hears her husband starting his motorcycle, she raises her voice and tells him, "On your way back, do not forget to buy fresh vegetables from the market." This is how the mind is in prayer. It is really difficult for the mind to remain silent and focus on God.

In prayer without words, we are called to take the risk in letting go of the familiar ground on which we stand and our usual style of praying, and enter into the world of deep silence. "But when you pray, go into your room and shut the door and pray to your Father who is in secret; and your Father who sees in secret will reward you. And in praying do not heap up empty phrases as the Gentiles do; ..." (Mt 6:6-7). Inner room and closing the door, refers not only to external silence, but also the inner silence. The body and mind with all of their faculties are directed to God alone. The mind in silence becomes aware of nothing except its presence before God. In this awareness nothing else matters, the mind does not wander, and if it does, it is brought to the awareness of God again.

Thus, the biblical call to be still and know God is not like the silence that we experience when we withdraw from the outside world and noise. It is not even a concentrated silence that is useful to focus on a project. It is also not the peaceful silence one experiences in nature, or when listening to soft and melodious music. It is not the awaited silence after a violent storm. It is not a silence of shock and fear from a tragedy and death. Biblical silence is a call to be still in both body and mind to know God. If *to know* is to enter into a personal and living relationship with God, then the only goal of the biblical silence is to have an experience of union and intimacy with the divine.

In prayer without words, thoughts are not dropped and the mind is not brought under control to arrive at a noble silence. Silence, however grand and beautiful it may be, still is not the goal of prayer. In the stillness and silence of the body and mind, we open our entire being, our mental and volitional faculties, to God alone and remain in God, letting every part of our being be filled with the grace and light of God. The focus of silence is not our selves, but God.

Silence results in the awareness of emptiness. Experience of emptiness is not negative, but essential for well-being and beauty of life. It is the empty space within musical notes that makes music possible and harmonious. It is the empty space between the flowers that make the bouquet of flowers so pleasing to the eye. From the circumference of the wheel, the spokes merge at the hub where there is only emptiness, and this emptiness is essential for the wheel to rotate. It is through the empty window that breeze and sunlight enter a room. Silence results in emptiness, but this emptiness in prayer without words is not a negative emptiness, but a positive emptiness. It is an emptiness that is not focused on itself, but open to God. It is an emptiness that is filled with God's presence. It is in this apparent emptiness that we experience God as the ground of our being.

Solitude

Moses did not encounter God in Pharaoh's palace in Egypt, but in the silence of the desert. From slavery to freedom, the people of Israel had to cross the desert. The prophets were called to the desert. People came to listen to John the Baptist in the desert. Jesus, after his own baptism, was led by the Spirit into the desert. During his public ministry Jesus chose mountains and deserts to pray in solitude. The desert refers to more than just a geographical expression, the desert also refers to a place of God's revelation, a place where God prepared his chosen ones, a place God spoke to his people, a place of God experience, a place where one was stripped of all false securities and had nothing to hold onto except God alone. It was a place of purification and a place to encounter God in silence.

The command to go to one's inner room and close the door (Mt 6:5-6) is an invitation to withdraw to quiet places, to our own deserts to be with God. Pope John Paul II once said, "We are so busy with the work of the Lord that we forget the Lord of the work." When Martha complained about Mary to Jesus, he said to her, "... Mary has chosen the good portion, which shall not be taken away from her" (Lk 10:42). We need to spend quality time alone with the Lord. Time spent in solitude is not only our wanting to be with God, but it is also God desiring to spend time exclusively with us. This can be possible only when we create our own deserts. We need to get away from our busy lifestyle, from the various and many activities of the day, even from the most satisfying spiritual ministries to be with the Lord.

Jesus' own prayer life stands out as a great model and example to be followed. Jesus' day was sandwiched between two moments of prayer in solitude. He began the day in silent prayer and ended his day in silent prayer in solitude. He either withdrew to the mountain or into the desert to pray. Throughout the day all that he said and did flowed from the communion that he experienced with his Father. "... The words that I say to you I do not speak on my own authority; but the Father who dwells in me does his works" (Jn 14:10). We withdraw into solitude to encounter, to be present to, and to experience oneness, intimacy, and union with God. In the desert we are renewed, purified, and strengthened by God to face the many challenges of our everyday life, and to bring the presence of God into the activities of the day and to our relationships. Someone recently said to me, "The entire message of the gospel is: *Come and go.*" How true! We withdraw to spring forth.

Experience

Prayer without words is not to arrive at an experience of feeling good or having nice feelings. It is not to reach absolute emptiness and to remain in that emptiness. It is not a journey of introspection. It is not to master altered states of consciousness. Faith tells us that we are in the presence of God and prayer is an experience of God. In this experience, I realize that although I am distinct from God, I am not separated from God since God is the ground of my existence. It is impossible to conceive of my life and my being outside of God. Not a single moment can I live severed from God, who is the source and foundation of my being. The scripture says, "for 'In him we live and move and have our being'; ..." (Acts 17:28). Whether I am conscious or not, I am always in God. In prayer without words we become aware that we are in God, we are in the presence of God and that we live, move, and have our being in God. In profound silence before God, the subject/object dichotomy and the knower and the act of knowing disappear and then only the known remains. Only God remains. Prayer is an experience of being with this "known alone."

With only our spiritual and theological words, we can never fully grasp the meaning of the invisible mystery, for every affirmation is a negation of God. God is a mystery to be lived and not a problem to be solved. Prayer is to let go of the desire to fix God into our neat categories and concepts; it is becoming aware and realizing that we are not separated from God. In prayer we are like earthen vessels, empty and awaiting to be filled with God's grace and light. Waiting in silence and in solitude is alien to our culture. We are result-oriented and we want it immediately. In waiting we realize we are powerless, we depend on someone other than ourselves. We do not call the shots. We totally surrender. We wait for God to act.

Prayer is an experience of dropping our false self and becoming aware and realizing the fundamental truth that God, as the ground of our being constitutes our true nature. "If any man would come after me, let him deny himself and take up his cross and follow me" (Mk 8:34). Prayer is losing the false self and realizing the true self, the Christ nature in us. Stillness leads to knowing God and as the awareness deepens, even the stillness and the realization of knowing disappear, and only God remains. In the awareness of God alone, we realize our true nature. It is an experience, and such an experience is possible for all who are prepared to invest time in prayer; prayer in silence, stillness, and solitude.

Prayer without words is also to experience oneness with all other beings. God is not only transcendent but also immanent. God's existence in the universe is not along with other existences, but God exists as the ground of all beings. Just as God is the ground of my being, so too, God is the ground of all beings. The experience of oneness with God leads to an experience of oneness with all other beings.

Christocentric

All prayers that are addressed to the Father are made through Christ. So, too, prayer without words is in and through the person of Christ. It is Christocentric. Jesus said to Thomas, "I am the way, and the truth, and the life; no one comes to the Father, but by me" (Jn 14:6). Jesus is the way to the Father. Jesus is the truth and the source of eternal life. We are not theists, but we believe in an incarnated God, a God who has reached out and has reconciled us through his Son, Jesus Christ. Christian revelation believes in the truth of mediation, God mediating through the person of Jesus. Jesus is the center and core of our spirituality.

When we drop the false ego in prayer without words, we become aware of our true self, and the true self is the very nature of Christ in us. St. Paul said, "I have been crucified with Christ; it is no longer I who live, but Christ who lives in me; ..." (Gal 2:20). In prayer we are united with Christ's nature in us, and it is through Christ that we pray to the Father. It is not a blind trust in a particular technique to arrive at silence and to remain in that silence, but in that silence, to let the Spirit cry out to God, "Abba, Father" for, "Out of the depths I cry to thee, O LORD!" (Ps 130: 1). In prayer without words, we are in the presence of God, and it is the Spirit that raises our hearts and minds to God. It is through the work of the Spirit that we learn to let go and surrender to God, trusting in God, and waiting upon God to act in us. Thus, it is not our own achievement, and we do not transform ourselves; but it is God's grace that brings about these changes in us. In prayer we let ourselves be transformed by Christ's paschal mystery, experiencing death and birth, birth into a new creation.

Known by its Fruit

How do we know that it is God experience and not self-induced? The criteria is given by Jesus himself: "... for the tree is known by its fruit" (Mt 12:33). St. Paul describes the fruit of the Spirit: "... love, joy, peace, patience, kindness, goodness, faithfulness, gentleness, self-control..." (Gal 5:22-23). It is not selfishness to be silent, to be withdrawn into solitude, and to be resting in God, but we allow the experience of God to penetrate our mental consciousness and activities of the day. All our responses and activities flow from the experience of divine intimacy. Prayer without words brings about a contemplative outlook on life. Opening oneself to God in silence is a liberating experience. It fills us with the fruit of the Spirit and these fruit characterize our values, habits, attitude, behavior, character, and actions. The fruit reveal the source, God. Jesus said to the apostles, "Believe me that I am in the Father and the Father in me; or else believe me for the sake of the works themselves" (Jn 14:11). What Jesus did flowed from his communion with his Father: "... The words that I say to you I do not speak on my own authority; but the Father who dwells in me does his works" (Jn 14:10).

The type of person that I want to be, is in turn, qualified by the person that I am. The experience of God in prayer reveals to me the person that I am. The more I experience God, the more I realize that my true and original nature is constituted by the very fruit of the Spirit, the very nature of Christ himself. Thus, we begin to realize that it is not that we do acts of compassion, but we become compassion itself, not that we do acts of nonviolence, but we become nonviolence itself, not that we do acts of forgiveness, but we become forgiveness itself, not that we do works of peace, but we become peace itself. There begins to appear the harmony between the inner and the outer. The outer begins to flow from the inner. What we do becomes an extension of who we are.

On a Practical Level
> ➢ Develop the habit of spending at least some time during the day in silence.
> ➢ Once a week, turn off the T.V. and the radio and just be with yourself.
> ➢ Once every few months spend one full day in total silence.
> ➢ Once a year attend a silent retreat.
> ➢ Try not to begin the day with the news in the media. Spend a few minutes in silent prayer/meditation at the beginning of the day.
> ➢ Create your own desert in your home and form the habit of retreating into the desert to spend time everyday in solitude for a few minutes.
> ➢ Learn to pray without words (Jesus Prayer, Centering Prayer, Meditation…)
> ➢ In your conversations learn to listen more and talk less.
> ➢ Remember: "Words are silver, but silence is golden."
> ➢ Form the habit of reading spiritual books.

> A man who had gone away on an extended business tour returned to his beloved's home and knocked on the door. "Who is it?" demanded the voice of his beloved from inside. "It is I" replied the man. She said, "There is no room here for me and you." The man departed thinking on the response of his beloved. After a couple of months he returned and knocked again on the door of his beloved. Again his beloved demanded, "Who is it?" He replied, "It is you." The door was immediately opened and he was in the arms of his beloved.
>
> —*A Sufi Story*

In the deep experience of prayer, everything disappears and only God remains.

Oh God!

Like the deer that longs for the running stream
and the sentry for the daybreak, so too my soul
longs for you my God.
Out of my depths I cry to you my God, come take
possession of me for I am incomplete without you.
I ask of you nothing my God, except the grace of
experiencing you.
Bless me with courage to enter into deep silence
and to be just in your loving presence doing nothing.
Increase my love for solitude and also the grace to
retreat into my desert everyday.

I have realized my God that nothing in this world will
ever satisfy the longings of my heart except you
and you alone, my God.
Come fill me, my heart, my soul, my mind, and my body.
I beg you for the grace of the experience of oneness,
intimacy, and union with you.
May your indwelling presence remain with me and may
I constantly return to be strengthened and nourished
by your loving presence that is always in me.

In silence and stillness of the body and mind,
in the experience of oneness, union, and
intimacy with God
we experience true self-realization.

Self: In Dropping It, You Will Find It

> *If any man would come after me,*
> *let him deny himself and*
> *take up his cross and follow me.*
> —Mk 8:34

> *You can give up various possessions.*
> *If, instead, you give up, 'I' and 'mine,'*
> *you give them all up in one stroke and*
> *lose the very seed of possession.*
> —Ramana Maharshi

At the beginning of the Eucharistic celebration as the priest greeted the congregation by saying, "The Lord be with you" he realized that something was wrong with the microphone. He turned to the acolyte and said to him, "Something is wrong with the microphone." The people responded, "And also with you."

There is something fundamentally wrong with the way in which we believe ourselves to be. One such strong belief is our understanding and perception of the nature of the self in us. What is the self? Is there a real self, and if there is, what is its nature? If self is denied then who am I? Why do religions insist on dropping the self to experience God? In the God experience what happens to the self? If the self is dropped, then who is the "I" that experiences God?

Jesus says, "... If any man would come after me, let him deny himself and take up his cross and follow me" (Mk 8:34). Again in the gospel of Matthew he says, "He who finds his life will lose it, and he who loses his life for my sake will find it" (Mt: 10:39). The true meaning of self, and consequently the true meaning of life, emerges in the apparent contradiction of *losing and finding*. What is this denial, losing and finding that Jesus is talking about? Something must be lost in order that something else can be found. It is only in denying and losing the self that we will find life. It is in the courage to let go of the perception of the self that we have of ourselves, that we will be able find our true self. True self is not discovered by dropping the ego, having a false sense of humility, low self-esteem, or through acts of self-denial, asceticism, and mortifications; but it is only in the dropping of the false self the true self emerges.

False Self

Day-to-day human experience points to the existence of the self, which is often expressed as *I, I am, Mine, Me*, and *Ego*. Observe the human language. Existence is identified with the self: *I am. This is I. This is how I am.* So too, at the level of feelings and emotions: *I am angry. I am upset. I am in love. I am happy. I am depressed...* Personal characteristics are expressed in terms of the self: *I am good. I am a sensate. I am an introvert. I am a thinker...* Self is identified with cultural, political, religious, professional, and social roles: *I am an American, I am an Asian, I am a Democrat, I am a Christian, I am a wife, I am a doctor, I am a mother, I am a friend...* A sense of possession comes along with the use of self. *This is my house, my car, and these are mine. This is my family, my nation, my job, my emotions, my thoughts, my feelings...* and the list of *mine* goes on endlessly. Is the self that is constantly identified with *I, Me,* and *Mine* the true self? We tend to think and believe it to be so.

Is my real self any of the above? Can my true self be identified with my emotions, feelings, body, mind, nationality, culture, religion, politics, social roles, profession, possessions, and relationship? There are no elements of stability or permanence in any of these. If self is identified with all that is transient, then self, too, should be constantly changing. There is nothing solid or substantial in what we normally perceive and understand the self to be.

The self that we think to be true is just a label used to indicate the body-mind structure. The problem arises when we take the label to be real, true, non-changing, and permanent rather than just seeing it as indicating the changing process of body-mind structure. It is an illusion to identify the self with the body-mind structure and all the various experiences that happen to and within the body-mind phenomena that is constantly changing.

An illusion is a false belief and not an erroneous perception. For example, to perceive a rope as a snake is a misperception and not a false belief, but to believe that "having more" is the secret of happiness is a false belief. We need to drop the greatest illusion of identifying the self with all that is transient and changing. Like peeling away the various layers of an onion, so too, we need to drop the various illusions to perceive the true nature of the self. Let us explore some of these illusions.

Can the self be identified with thoughts? Can I ask, "Are these *my* thoughts?" "*Am I* my thoughts?" Can the self be reduced to thoughts that rise and fall, over which we have no control? We do not invite them. They come and disappear on their own. In prayer without words we are just aware of their rising and falling. One thought replaces another. When new thoughts have replaced old thoughts, where is the self that is identified with these thoughts? Has the self also changed? Self is not thoughts that arise and fall.

Is it possible to identify the self with various experiences that happen to us? Can I ask, "Are these experiences *mine? Am I* my experiences?" Is the self a total sum of all our experiences? We have a variety of experiences. Some are strong and others weak. Some we remember and some we forget. Memories of past experiences remain; sometimes even the feelings that accompanied the experience, but not with the same intensity. Experiences, like thoughts, come and go. One experience replaces another. Self cannot be permanently identified with experiences that are constantly changing.

What about feelings and emotions? Can the self be identified with them? "*Am I* my feelings and emotions?" Am I the totality of all the various feelings and emotions that have ever happened to me? What is the nature of feelings and emotions? They too, like thoughts and experiences constantly change and are unpredictable. We begin the day with the decision to be happy, but soon we find ourselves grouchy, sad, angry, upset, and depressed. What has happened to our happy feelings? They change. They change for various reasons. Certain causes come together and give rise to certain feelings, and when the causes disappear, the feelings disappear also. There is no permanence in them. Self cannot be identified with that which is transient.

How about the body? Can I ask, "Is my body my *self?*" "A*m I* my body?" Experience reveals that the body is not permanent either. Over the years the body has also changed. Some cells have died, some are renewed, and new ones are born. There is constant change in the body. The body goes through various stages: fetus, infancy, childhood, teenage, adulthood, middle age, and old age; one stage giving way to another. Self cannot be identified with the body at its several different stages because the body is constantly changing.

The same holds true for our mind. Self cannot be reduced to the mind, for the contents of the mind are constantly changing. There is not just one thought that occupies the mind, but thousands of thoughts that flash across the mind. It is no wonder that the mind is called the "monkey mind" for it is never at rest. Can the self be identified with all the thoughts that arise and fall in the mind? When thoughts cease, what is the nature of the mind and where is it? Does the self disappear too?

Self is not defined by what we possess. The nature of the self is not determined by the vehicle I possess, the house that I live in, the bank balance that I have, the fancy clothes that I wear, and the places I have visited. We are stewards of God's creation. God has entrusted us with responsibility for the material goods of this world, and for all that we have and possess. We have them for sometime. Today it is mine and tomorrow it belongs to someone else. It is never fully mine. At death we leave everything behind except the fruit of our true "self."

So too, the true self cannot be identified with social, religious, political, cultural, and professional roles: being a son, a friend, a husband, a parent, a believer, an Indian, or a capitalist. The different roles that we assume are time determined and we assume different roles during our lives. Roles that we assume change also and there is no permanence in them; the self cannot be reduced to one particular role.

The process of identifying something as permanent, is living in the past and refusing to live in the present. Are we the sum total of our past? What about the present and the vast future that is open before us?

Heraclitus, the Greek philosopher, used to say that one cannot take a bath twice in the same river because the water is constantly moving. There is constant movement and change in the universe. Apparent solid matter consists of particles constantly interacting with one another and in that process, replacing the old and giving birth to new ones. Perception, without awareness, comes into contact only with appearance and not with the reality itself. Our common perception is one of solidity, and such a perception determines and qualifies our view of reality. We believe solidity to be the ultimate truth of reality and hold onto it because we do not experience reality as constantly changing and in a state of flux. Just as we believe in the illusion of appearances while watching a film, because the frames of a film move at a rapid speed, so too, we perceive the appearance to be real and not the reality itself.

When we look within, into our own body and mind, we experience the truth of impermanence and the transient nature of reality. When in deep silence, we become aware of the various sensations in the body, we realize the transient nature of sensations that rise and fall. Sensations, whether pleasant or unpleasant, are never permanent. They are constantly changing and in a state of flux. Impermanence accompanies every sensation in our bodies. When awareness is more refined, the body that in fact appears to be solid, is in truth constantly changing. Sensations rise and fall. New ones come and they too pass. Where is the self that is in control of these sensations? Is it really me? Am I really my sensations? Can we attach an unchanging self to these sensations? There really is no solid, unchanging self that is the owner of these sensations. This is true not only with regard to sensations, but also to all other experiences that occur within the body-mind structure. Gautama Buddha used to say:

> When you see, let there be just seeing; when
> you hear a sound, let there be just hearing;
> when you smell an odor, let there be just
> smelling; when you taste a flavor, let there be
> just tasting; when you experience a
> sensation, let there be just sensing; and
> when a thought arises, let it be just a natural
> phenomenon arising in the mind. When it is
> like this, there will be no self, there will be no
> moving about here and there, and no
> stopping anywhere.

We are not really who and what we think ourselves
to be. The self that we normally understand to be, is
only a label to indicate the mind-body structure and
the various mental-physical experiences that happen
within this structure. Different sense experiences:
seeing, smelling, tasting, touching, hearing, and
mental experiences such as thoughts and emotions
occur in the mind-body structure that we call "me" and
"mine." These different experiences occur in the mind-
body person that we are, stay for a while and
disappear. There is nothing permanent in them, but
mistakenly we posit an unchanging self onto them,
and falsely identify the self with them, thinking and
believing that our true self is in all of these
experiences. The different experiences are like different
scenes that are projected on the screen. The screen
does not identify itself with the images that are
projected on it. The mirror reflects the different objects

held in front of it, but the mirror itself does not identify with what it reflects.

Through the association of various concepts we can construct ideas of things, but they are only ideas and not reality itself. In a similar manner, the mind constructs an unchanging permanent self, but such a self exists only in the mind. The self, created by the mind, is an idea of ourselves that does not correspond to who we really are. The "I" that we mistakenly think to be the true self is only a label to indicate the mind-body structure and not the truth of who we really are. The true self can never be identified with the mental-physical processes that are constantly changing and are always in a state of flux. With awareness we perceive that each experience is an experience that rises and falls, and the work of identifying the self with these experiences is done by the mind. Ramana Maharshi, the great mystic, used to say that when we drop the mind and when we remain still, we experience self-realization. In other words, when the mind stops the process of identification, we then begin to perceive the true nature of the self.

True self

"No self" or the call to deny one's self is not truly a denial of self. It is only in dropping the false self that the true self emerges. The true self is within us. We don't have to invent it, or posit it, or identify it with passing and changing experiences. In the correct perception of who we are, we will understand the nature of our true self.

In the first place, stop identifying the self with all the various experiences happening to the mind-body structure as "This is *me*," "This *is mine*," and "This is *myself*." Observe experiences for what they really are. Do not identify the self with them. Realize that there is no solid, unchanging self that is to be found in all the different mental-physical processes.

The second truth to realize is that what happens to the mind-body structure are just experiences; different experiences arising and falling, none of which are permanent and unchanging. Understand the experiential truth that when various causes come together, certain experiences occur as a result. When the causes disappear, the effect disappears, too. There is no self that is causing these experiences to happen. It is very important to understand this truth because the true self is not in these experiences. And if we mistakenly identify the true self with what is happening both to the body and mind, then the self is also constantly changing because these experiences by nature are bound to change.

Ramana Maharshi taught that true self realization is answering the most important question, *"Who am I?"* If by process of elimination we discard all that is not the true self, then we arrive at the true self. According to Ramana Maharshi, all that we need to do is to *"be still and realize the true self."* In stillness and silence we experience the biblical truth that we are created in the image and likeness of God. We are filled with the very breath of God, the Spirit of God. The core of our existence is constituted by the very presence of God within us. God is the ultimate foundation of our existence. For Paul Tillich, God is the depth of life, the ultimate concern, the source of our being, and the depth and ground of all being. God is not an existence alongside other existences, but God is the ground of all existence. According to Karl Rahner, God is the ultimate depth and radical essence of every human experience. These human experiences that serve as "signals of transcendence" point to the mystical center within us. The deepest human experiences enable us to acknowledge the presence of God within us, who is the core, the center, and the ground of our existence. It is only in God, as the Bible says, that we live, move, and have our being. It is impossible to conceive of our existence apart from God.

In the previous chapter, I emphasized that in prayer without words we transcend the normal mental consciousness and we reach a depth where the unitive consciousness, transcending all forms of dualities, is present to the presence of God. This unitive consciousness, transcending all dualities, experiencing oneness, intimacy, and union with God, is our original nature, the original blessing, and as Zen says, "the face that I had before I was born." This is the true self, the self that does not identify itself with the passing and changing things that the mind-body structure experiences. The true self is the self that is constantly before, and living in, the indwelling presence of God. The nature of the self is to realize itself in the experience of intimacy, union, and oneness with God. The nature of our true self is to experience what Jesus experienced, "I and the Father are one" (Jn 10:30). The self that transcends all dualities, divisions, and separations, and is united with God and God alone, is the true self. Only in this oneness, intimacy, and union with God is the nature of the self-revealed. It is being in the presence of God and resting in God that self finds its meaning.

In this experience of oneness with God, the self is dependent on God alone. The self, apart from God, is empty and only in the presence of God, and filled with the presence of God, does it become real. Its reality is its non-separatedness from God. In the deep experience of God, the self not only becomes aware of its non-separatedness from God, but also experiences oneness with all other beings, because God alone is the foundation of all beings.

For Advaita-Vedanta *Tat Tvam Asi* (Thou Art That) is the core of self-realization. Advaita-Vedanta perceives Brahman as the ultimate reality, the core, and inner essence of all things. Brahman is the sole reality; whatever is, is Brahman. In Brahman, all distinctions and contradictions disappear. The atman (the self) is the manifestation of Brahman in the individual. The atman and Brahman are one in essence, and self-realization is realizing the most basic and foundational truth that atman and Brahman are one.

Brahman alone is real, and real implies that which is permanent, eternal, infinite, that which is *trikalabadhyam* (never substituted at any time by another experience). In contrast to Brahamn, all other realities lack fullness of being. Only Brahman is real and everything else is *maya* (illusion). Maya is the erroneous perception that perceives the constantly changing world as real.

Self-realization is experiencing the truth that atman and Brahman are one, the identification of the self with the Self. The *mahavakyas* (the great sayings) *Tat Tvam Asi* (Thou Art That) *Aham Brahma Asmi* (I am Brahman) *Ayam atma Brahma* (This atman is Brahamn) are central truths of Advaita-Vedanta. To merge and become one with the Self is the goal of true realization, because for Advaita-Vedanta there is only one consciousness and it is the Absolute Consciousness in us. In self-realization the subject-object dichotomy disappears, as well as the dichotomy between the knower and the known and only the known remains. As in a dance the dancer disappears and only the dance remains; as in singing the singer disappears and only the song remains; so too in self-realization, only God remains.

For the Persian mystics, the self is a spark of the divine and self-realization is the experience of the divine. For the Taoists too, the ultimate goal of life is to merge with a True Self. True Self is the only thing that is real and everything else is in continuous flow and change. The Buddhists speak of no self and emptiness. "Being nobody and going no where" is a Buddhist expression that captures the true meaning of self. To drop the self, emptiness of the self does not mean that there is no self. True self is the experience that the self is not separated from the ground of existence of life.

True self is not to identify with the passing things of this world and life. It is pure *awareness.* Emptiness is not a state of nothingness, but the source of all life. In the experience of emptiness, the self is connected to everything else in the universe. Following Thich Nhat Hanh's understanding of "interbeing," we can say that a tiny leaf is nothing, yet it contains all the elements and forces of nature within it. The leaf in being nothing, contains everything.

Religions differ in their notion of God, nature of self-realization, beliefs, and expression of their beliefs, but they all converge on the truth that self-realization is experience of oneness with God (the source of life). Self and self-realization cannot be identified with the changing things of this world, or with the physical-mental processes, but only with God, who alone is real. Self is the most fundamental nature in us and God is the very foundation of that nature. It is only when we think that we are independent of God, the notion of false self emerges. Sin is the experience of separation, dichotomy, alienation, and division between self and its source of life, God. Apart from God, the self does not exist and does not realize its truth.

Search for the true self is a journey to the very source of our life. It is a journey that begins with the courage to drop the false self, the world of appearances, to behold God alone, and to be with and in God's presence. In God's presence the true self is without selflessness and without ego. Self in its deepest core is an experience of the "original blessings," "the rediscovering of the face that we had before we were born," "being born again in the Spirit;" it is reaching the depth of God experience, where we can say like St. Paul, "I have been crucified with Christ; it is no longer I who live, but Christ who lives in me; ..." (Gal 2:20). What does it mean to have Christ's nature in us? It is a nature, where in its depth, the self out of its experience of oneness, divine intimacy, and union with God understands the truth of the greatest *mahavakya,* "I and the Father are one" (Jn 10:30).

Jesus' True Self

John Martin Sahajananda in his, *You Are The Light, Rediscovering the Eastern Jesus* speaks of four different "I's" of Jesus. The first is the individual *I* of Jesus as a human being determined by his personal consciousness. The second *I* is the consciousness of Jesus conditioned by his Jewish identity and the spiritual tradition of which he was a part. The third *I* of Jesus is the consciousness of Jesus that was open to the transcendent mystery of God, a consciousness that leads him to the experience of himself as the Son of the Father. The fourth *I* of Jesus is the consciousness where Jesus experienced oneness, intimacy, and union with the Father, and out of this union he was able to say, "I and the Father are one" (Jn 10:30).

The true self in Jesus, transcending all forms of dualities, longed for the intimacy, union, and oneness with his Father. It was the self that experienced a unitive consciousness that constantly strived to live in the presence of his Father. It was this self that reached out and related to everyone and everything around him. Theologically, we speak of the hypostatic union in Christ and rightly so, but it was also a nature in which the self as the most basic foundational principle experienced total and absolute oneness with the Father, "I and the Father are one" (Jn 10:30). Just as Jesus experienced oneness with the Father, he prayed that we too, experience oneness with the Father. It is this experience of oneness, and divine intimacy with God that really defines and qualifies the nature of our true self. When the self realizes oneness with the Father, when we begin to live from the center, when what we do begins to flow from what we are, when our light begins to shine and salt has its saltiness, then we live the Christ nature in us. It is only when the self stops identifying itself with the *maya(s)* of this world, and when it transcends all forms of dualities and is in union with God, does it realize its true nature, the Christ nature.

The scholastic metaphysical principle states, "As a being is, so it acts." The other principle is also equally true, "Acts reveal the nature of the being." Acts reveal the nature of the self and a particular self is revealed by its acts. Jesus lived and acted from the center, from his experience of oneness with the Father: "Truly, truly, I say to you, the Son can do nothing of his own accord, but only what he sees the Father doing; for whatever he does, that the Son does likewise" (Jn 5:19-20). Experience of the Father was the foundation of his life, mission, words, and deeds. In the opening prayer of the Seventh Sunday the Church prays, "That we may imitate the words and actions of Jesus." As his disciples, through a life of spiritual discipline, we are called to "imitate the words and actions of Jesus."

In the Steps of Jesus

Jesus' true self is manifested in his words and actions:

> ➤ Humility is a nature of the self: "who, though he was in the form of God, did not count equality with God a thing to be grasped, but emptied himself, taking the form of a servant, being born in the likeness of men" (Phil 2:6-7).
> ➤ Jesus did not identify his self with the material things, riches, glory, and the promises of the devil, but with God alone (Mt 3:1-11). Neither did Jesus identify his self with the religious and social aristocracies, nor with the political powers of his time. The more his reputation grew, the more he sought the experience of union and intimacy with God.
> ➤ Jesus did not identify his self with what others thought about him (Mt 16:13-17).
> ➤ When people were looking for Jesus after the multiplication of the loaves, Jesus tells them to search for the food that endures for eternal life (Jn 6:26-27). Such a life lived by the self is glorifying God on earth and in heaven.
> ➤ True self is not selfish. It is prepared to let go of the bliss of a most beautiful experience in order to share the truth, the way, and the life so that others may experience similar bliss for themselves. While Peter, John, and James wanted to stay on the mountain after The

Transfiguration of Jesus, Jesus returned to the plains (Lk 9:28-36).

➤ True self is selfless and self-giving. It always thinks of others and their well-being even to the point of pain, suffering, and sacrifice of oneself (Jn 15:13).

➤ Self is not identified with what we do, or accomplish, but its true nature is to be living in the presence of God. It is enjoying the contemplative gaze at God (Lk 10:40-42).

➤ Love that emanates from the true self is not parochial, or regional, but universal. It reaches out to everyone, going beyond caste, creed, color, and community. Everyone is my neighbor (Lk 10:29-37). Its love is unconditional (Lk 15).

➤ Compassion is the cornerstone of the true self. Compassion is a stir, a movement in the heart of the person. It refuses to be indifferent in the face of need and suffering (Lk 7:13; Mt 14:14).

➤ Self experiences happiness, peace, and joy that are not by products of doing or having something, but they are a state of being. They come from within, flowing from the center (Mt 5:3-11).

➤ Self does not judge or condemn others (Jn 8). It is not jealous (I Cor 13:4). Its nature is forgiveness (Lk 23:34) and nonviolent (Mt 26:52). Nonviolence is not a choice, but the very essence of the self. Self is free and spacious, hence it can relate to all both rich and poor, righteous and sinners.

Jesus did not identify his true self with what others considered to be true. Jesus, as the gospel of John portrays, was one who longed and realized deep communion with his Father. Out of this experience of oneness with God, he was able to say: "... I am in the Father and the Father in me; ... (Jn 14:10); "I and the Father are one" (Jn 10:30); "... He who has seen me has seen the Father; ..." (Jn 14:9). From his experience of the Father he knew that the nature of the self is to be living in, and to be with, God; and that the true identity of the self is realized only in the experience of oneness with the Father. It is for this reason he retreats into silence and solitude. His life, words, and acts flowed from the realization and awareness of his true self-centered in God. When St. Paul reminds us to pray constantly and ceaselessly, it is "to move, live, and have" our life with the continuous awareness of being present to God, being grounded in God, being non-separated from God, and that true self-realization is possible only in the experience of oneness, union, and divine intimacy with God. It is in this experience we realize our true nature, "Christ's nature" in us.

A man was searching for something near a street lamp. A police officer passing by stopped and asked him what he was doing. He said, "I lost my house key. I am searching for it." The officer, wanting to help him, joined him in the search. Not finding the key, the officer asked him, "Where exactly did you lose the key?" The man replied, "Near my house." "Then why are you searching for the key here?" asked the officer. The man replied, "Because there is more light here."

Where are we searching for our true self?

Oh God!

All my life I have been identifying my "self" with the changing and passing things of this world.

Open my eyes to the truth that my true "self" can never be identified with material things, my body, and my mind.

Bless me with the grace to know, accept, and live the truth, that the self does not exist apart from you, for you are the only reality and everything else is maya.

My Lord, I ask for nothing except the grace of the experience of oneness with you, for it is only in this experience I will realize my "self."

It is only in you that "I live, move, and have my being."

Give me the gift of divine intimacy and union with you my God.

That I too, can say, "It is no longer I who live, but Christ who lives in me."

May the constant awareness of Christ's nature in me be in all that I say and do.

In meditation,
which is being still and knowing God
the self realizes its true nature.

Be Still: The Joy of Meditation

Be still, and know that I am God...
—Psalm 46:10

Learn to be silent.
Let your quiet mind listen and absorb.
—Pythagoras

The "Why" of Meditation

The thought of meditation can bring up several images: The Tibetan monks lying on icy snow in the Himalayas, the yogis contorting their limbs into unimaginable positions, people sitting quietly for hours doing nothing, seemingly enjoying deep peaceful silence, monks with wires hooked up to their heads to study the numerous positive effects of meditation on the human brain, Zen koans and Zen stories, esoteric pictures of Tantric meditation, people sacrificing their well deserved holidays to attend meditation retreats, these and other images; both positive and negative crop up into our imaginations.

Often, many are of the opinion that meditation is only for those who have renounced the world, for those who have a mystical view about life, for those who have nothing to achieve, to accomplish, or to look forward to in life, and for people who have transcended all emotions and morality. Some may even believe that meditation is not for the common everyday people who are racing against time to get things done, for those who climb the ladder of success, for those who have a family to care for, jobs to go to, things to be seen to, mortgages to be paid, vacations to be planned, new homes to be bought, etc. They may come to the conclusion that meditation isn't for those who have thousands of things to do. Furthermore, they may wonder, why expose themselves to meditation that is often and mistakenly identified as the oriental stuff?

Still others may feel that meditation is a waste of their precious time when there are so many other activities they could be engaging in and one life is not enough to get them all completed. When people are suffering and when there are so many issues of injustices, can one afford to be indifferent by sitting in silence? Why bother to sit agonizingly in a lotus position, putting up with pain and agony, to enjoy a few moments of bliss when intoxicants and substances can easily result in an altered state of consciousness? Meditation may sometimes appear to be a denial of life and all that life can bring to us. It is much easier to be a couch potato. For many people it is far more relaxing to sit with pretzels and beer and watch T.V. than to sit in meditation. Isn't it more enjoyable to watch movies, socialize, have drinks, go to a party, and gossip rather than achieve stillness and silence? Some may feel that they do not have any problems and, therefore, why meditate?

Let us be honest with ourselves. Are we really close to God? Are we really experiencing God? Jesus, in the gospels says, "I and the Father are one" (Jn 10:30). For

Jesus, prayer is entering into communion with God. Do we really desire to enter into this communion and truly experience God as Jesus did? Doesn't he expect the same, the experience of God from his disciples? Isn't it true that most of our training and devotion is limited to the mind? Why is God only an idea in our mind? Does our heart enter into our prayer experience? True prayer becomes an expression of love only when it arises from the heart. The Bible teaches, "Be still, and know that I am God..." (Ps 46:10), but why is it so difficult to be still, both in mind and body? We may be satisfied being devotionally religious, but are we really spiritual? We may be religious out of obligation; but in reality isn't religion reduced to a few religious practices: Sunday obligations, novenas, burning candles, (or we may be good Lenten Christians).

If people are truly religious, then why is forgiveness so difficult? Even when one claims to have forgiven unconditionally, why do past hurts still continue to control our lives and our behavior? If someone has genuinely forgiven the other person, why do people continue to believe that to forgive is easy, but to be able to forget is so very difficult? Why is there still so much anger and hatred in the human hearts?

The number of people suffering from depression is on the rise. We live, but is there life in our lives? Isn't there any freedom from stress, tension, and depression? Deep inside we do realize that several of our illnesses are psychosomatic in nature. Are we leading a satisfactory, contented, and happy life? Are we able to cope with different problems that arise in life? Are our relationships meaningful? Why do we often deviate from the focus and vision of our life? Why do we seem to lose the passion and energy for life? At the slightest provocation why do we explode like volcanoes? Why do we seem to easily lose our tempers? Why is our emotional life on a roller coaster? Why are we unable to remain calm and to think clearly in the face of difficulties, problems, and crises? Why do we always react rather than respond in freedom? Why do we need external stimulants to make us temporarily happy and to achieve peace? Isn't happiness often mistakenly identified with pleasures in life? Why is it so difficult to live in the present moment? Isn't it true that we either live in the past or in the future and hardly ever in the present moment, and yet we know that life is only in the present moment?

I am sure there are many other questions in our minds for which we have not yet been able to find satisfying answers. We would do anything to have our dissatisfactions, problems, worries, anxieties, stress, unhappiness, and tensions disappear. Each of us longs for peace and true happiness. We try various methods that seem to work temporarily, but soon we are back at the beginning. We seem to be happy for some time, but soon we will see through ourselves. We can become workaholics, but soon the activities that we believe to be so important become meaningless. There are some people who are hesitant to return home, not knowing how to spend time at home. The crucial question for them is, "What will I do today?"

Some pass their time shopping, and shopping for some has become so compulsive that they buy just for the sake of buying. Yet others wander aimlessly wasting precious time for the sake of not wanting to be at home. Others might spend their entire evening in front of the T.V. Still others keep themselves busy for the sake of keeping themselves busy. It is frightening. What happens when we are not able to do anything; does life come to an end? We put up a good front, but for how long? I am convinced that deep down inside all of us there must be another way to live our life. But we are either afraid or too lazy to take the plunge to discover other ways.

God-experience, peace, joy, contentment, and happiness are what every religion and society promises. It is for these that we invest our time in religious practices and work to have a comfortable life; but the irony is, even as we work, don't we often think of an early retirement, or working for the sake of the pay check, or just anticipating the week-end? Can our elected governments give us inner peace and happiness? Everyday the mental hospitals are being filled with more patients; old prisons are filled to over flowing, and new ones are being constructed. Didn't we witness the worst terrorist attack in human history at the beginning of this century? Our children are not even safe in our schools. Aren't we at each other's throats all in the name of caste, creed, color, community, and culture? Aren't we practicing subtle forms of discrimination? Aren't we witnessing a degeneration of values in our society? Are we not full of ego and a sense of false self? Something is certainly wrong. We are searching for a black cat in a dark room. We are searching for happiness and peace in the wrong places.

The Goal of Meditation

I am not suggesting that meditation is the panacea for all of the problems and afflictions in our life, our society, and the world at large, nor am I suggesting we fool ourselves into thinking that meditation is the only answer. Definitely there are several other spiritual paths. Each one has to find one's own spiritual path. I am strongly convinced that meditation can not only enable us to cope with our life and its problems, but can also lead us to true inner happiness and peace. Daily practice of meditation can result in many physical, psychological, mental, emotional, and spiritual benefits. *The greatest benefit is the life of union with and experience of God. Meditation is to be still and to know God. To know God is to have a personal intimate union with God, and through that experience, life and relationships become more beautiful and meaningful.*

In his prayer life Jesus as a pious Jew, would have prayed three times a day. As already pointed out (chapter on prayer), Jesus went to temples and synagogues with his disciples and other Jewish people. The gospels also present a Jesus who seems to have spent a lot of time praying in solitude. In the early mornings and late evenings he was found alone in prayer. He prayed on the mountaintops or in the deserts so that he would not be disturbed by anyone. Often, I wonder whether Jesus used a lot of words in these moments of prayer in solitude. St. Teresa of Avila said, "Prayer is to be with the one who loves us." I strongly believe that for Jesus, the time he spent with his heavenly Father were moments and experiences of intimate love and union. For Jesus, it was just being in love, remaining in love, being in that eternal joy and bliss which transcends all time, space, words, and concepts. Prayer for Jesus was a deep experience of God. Let us not be content with mental prayer and mere repetition of words, but let us strive for the ultimate, the God experience itself.

The goal of meditation is not to arrive at silence and stillness, but to be still and silent, to know God and to enter into communion with God. God experience, peace, and happiness are not out there to be found. They are within us, within our reach. The Reign of God is within us. Each one of us has to undertake this inner journey to discover and experience the Reign of God for ourselves and within ourselves. Religions, gurus, spiritual masters, saints, and religious leaders can only point the way to the truth, but each one of us has to embark on the journey by ourselves. The words in the scriptures point to God, but we seem to be contented with words, and not the reality the words point to. Meditation can take us to a level of experience, an experience of God, where words and concepts are dropped.

Young Mulla Nasrudin had a dream; he saw an old rabbi sitting on a vast pile of treasures in a farmhouse.

The rabbi told Nasrudin, "Come, take possession of the treasure that belongs to you." He was also given the address where the old rabbi lived. Thanking God for this great fortune that would soon become his, he set out immediately on his journey in search of his treasure. On the way he was robbed, beaten, sold into slavery, and almost killed. Finally, as a middle-aged man, he found the farmhouse and the old rabbi sitting on a bench just as he had seen in his dream. He was filled with joy to have reached his treasure. The old rabbi looked up at him and said, "Finally you have come. You are the one I saw in a dream I had many years ago. In my dream I saw you sitting on a chair, and underneath the chair there was a big pile of treasure. I wanted to go and find you, but due to my busy life I could never undertake the journey." When Nasrudin heard the old rabbi, it dawned on him that what he had been looking for all of his life, the treasure, was always within his own deepest self. The young man had the treasure within him, but he had to undertake such a difficult and dangerous journey to realize the truth. The treasure was within his reach, but he was searching for it outside himself.

It is also said that God did not want to be disturbed by the mortals. Hence, God asked the angels to suggest places where the mortals would not find God. One angel said, "God, you should hide on top of the highest mountain." God replied, "No, even there, they will find me." "How about the deepest ocean?" asked another angel. "No, with their latest submarines they will track me down," God replied. And so the conversation continued. Finally a little angel said, "God, why don't you hide in the hearts of the humans? They will never find you there." That's what God did, and that's where God has been and remains. That will be the last place where the human being will ever look for God.

Once we are in touch with the presence of God who is within us, we will know the truth and the truth will set us free. Unfortunately our essential and true self is hidden from us by various veils of illusion. We continue to believe in the reality of these illusions. We have forgotten who we are; we identify our true and original nature with our possessions and with what others tell us about ourselves. We do not have the time, patience, or the interest to get in touch with ourselves. We dogmatically believe what others tell us about who we are and what we should be.

The most difficult journey is the inward journey. We are so busy searching for God and peace everywhere that we are unable to realize that each one of us is a spark of the divine, and it is only in realizing this truth, that we will be able to find true happiness. The truth is not out there, but it is within us. We need to be in touch with the source that is in each one of us. Daily practice of meditation is one of the best ways of removing many illusions that cover our true nature.

In letting go of our false self, we can discover the true self. In Thailand when vacating a monastery, the monks came across a big statue covered with dirt and dust in the basement. Since it was a useless statue, they placed it outside the building. The following morning, to their surprise, in the place of the statue covered with dirt and dust, they saw the statue of a golden Buddha. During the night the rain had washed off the dirt and dust from the statue, thus revealing the golden Buddha. All along, the monks had the statue with them, never realizing the worth and the value of the statue made of gold. When the dirt and dust were removed, the original metal of the statue began to shine forth. Most of us believe that we are created in the image and likeness of God. Each one of us is a spark of the divine and eternal light. This is our true and original nature, the Christ nature in us. Due to sins, habits of sin, and because of various mental negativities and ignorance, layers of dust and dirt have accumulated and clouded our true nature from shining forth. We are disconnected from our true self. Our life, actions, and relationships do not stem forth from our true nature. Like the dark clouds that prevent the rays of the sun from reaching the earth, so too, our false ego, sins, and negativities prevent the true self from shining forth. Through the practice of meditation, we slowly and steadily remove layers and layers of dust; once the dust is removed, the true golden self begins to shine forth. We really do not have to make an effort to discover the true self. It is there. All that we need to do for the true self to shine forth, is to remove the dust and to drop the false self.

Probably the most difficult thing is to be silent and still. Pythagoras, who lived c. 500 B.C. said, "Learn to be silent. Let your quiet mind listen and absorb." Our culture doesn't seem to encourage the practice of meditation and silence. Also our mind constantly tells us that everything is fine with us. Our rational and logical mind can deceive us so easily. We live in a dream world not wanting to challenge and question the quality of our own life. Either we want to remain in misery or continue to fool ourselves that everything is all right with us. How difficult, demanding, and challenging it can be to sit quietly and listen to ourselves!

Some Common Excuses

One of the major objections to meditation is that one can't find time to meditate. The real issue is not finding time, but prioritizing our values, needs, and time. If inner transformation, peace, happiness, God experience, meaningful and fulfilling relationships, and an equanimous mind become a priority in our life, then we will definitely find time. When the body is sick, don't we find time to take care of it? If the body needs exercise, don't we find time to step into a gym or go for walks? If the doctor requests that I be admitted into the hospital, however busy I am, won't I make time? Similarly, when the mind is sick and continues to live in sickness, we should and need to take time to look after it. Ultimately, it is a question of priority and where one's interests lie.

We take good care of our bodies, but not our minds. Most of us, in the morning, are probably in the habit of taking a shower to purify and cleanse our body. We want our bodies to be fresh and alive. Before we leave home, we cleanse our bodies, spray on perfume, and do all that is necessary to make the skin shine. Also in the evening, after a long, hard day at work, we may be in the habit of taking a shower to feel fresh and to remove the dirt to which our bodies have been exposed throughout the day. We tend to take such good care of our bodies, but little do we realize that we also need to care for our minds as well. Both the body and the mind constitute the human person. Throughout the day there is much dust, dirt, mental irritants, thoughts, and negativities that gather in our mind. We retire to bed without purifying our mind, and in the morning we take time to purify our body but not our mind. We begin the day with much accumulated dirt and dust in our minds. We fail to feel the need and necessity to purify our mind. Daily practice of meditation not only purifies the mind, but also cleanses the mind of all the psychic irritants and mental negativities, things such as greed, hatred, lust, resentment, jealousy, envy, anger, depression, stress, tension, negative attitudes, and feelings, things that prevent us from living our life to the fullest. Daily purification of the mind brings the mind to a state of awareness, peace, clarity, tranquility, and eventually paves the way for God experience.

We seem to be afraid to take the plunge into silence and solitude, maybe because we are afraid to change. The closer we get to the fire the more it will burn, for that is the nature of fire. God told Moses, "Do not come near; put off your shoes from your feet, for the place on which you are standing is holy ground" (Ex 3:5). The more we become close to God, the more we will have to surrender our various sandals. Surrendering is very difficult. Surrendering creates an emptiness and silence within ourselves, and it is precisely this emptiness and silence that we are afraid of facing. To let go of ourselves, our ego, our false sources of happiness and to let God in, is very difficult. It is precisely this letting go of ego and letting God in that happens in our meditation practice.

We are frightened because God experience calls for change and transformation that we are sometimes not ready to make. It calls for a change of life style, change of attitudes, letting go of things that do not matter to us any longer, and changes in our character. After heart surgery when the doctor prescribes a change in our life style (activities, medications, food habits, etc.), we don't argue with the doctor. We are prepared to make the necessary changes in our life style because we want to live. Similarly, when we come close to God, God expects us to change for the better. Isn't it for our own well-being and happiness? Meditation becomes the sacred place where these changes can take place.

As stated above, most of us are somewhat afraid to take this inward journey for the fear of discovering what we may learn about ourselves. The macrocosm is the reflection of the microcosm. That is, what is going on outside is the reflection of what is going on inside each individual. Just as the mirror is capable of reflecting only what is held in front of it, so too, our life will reflect only that which is within each one of us. Our words, deeds, actions, decisions, and relationships reflect what is within us. The external is the manifestation of the internal. At times, don't we realize how our energy can affect others? When we are happy, our happiness spreads and affects the ambience. When we are sad, sadness tends to fill the room where we are. When we are grumpy, doesn't it influence the environment? If there is so much hatred and violence going on outside, it is because we are filled with violence, anger, and hatred within. One cannot commit murder unless the person generates a tremendous amount of anger and hatred within oneself, and one cannot commit rape unless one is filled with lust in one's heart. Didn't Jesus say that if one looks at another person with lust in one's heart, the person has already committed adultery in one's heart (Mt 5:27-28)? Daily practice of meditation not only enables us to be in touch with our deepest true self, but also makes us constantly aware of our thoughts, intentions, and the presence of ego in our relationships with others. Relationships are much like mirrors; they genuinely reflect the people that we are.

When a wound is cut open, it is then that the foul puss will come out. If one prefers to live with the wound, not only that part of the body will be amputated, but soon one will lose one's life as well. Similarly, when we go deep within ourselves, many thoughts and feelings will surface, and it is through meditation we not only become aware of these, but we also will learn to let go of them and soon they lose their power over us. Jesus said, "... for you are like whitewashed tombs, which outwardly appear beautiful, but within they are full of dead men's bones and all uncleanness. So you also outwardly appear righteous to men, but within you are full of hypocrisy and iniquity" (Mt 23:27-28). In meditation we learn to look within, and the outer flows from the inside. Soon there will be a perfect balance and harmony between the outer and the inner.

Daily practice of meditation will certainly give us an integrated approach to reality, to perceive beauty wherever it is found, to be fully present in each and every experience, to have a life of well-being, focused vision, needed energy to realize the vision, fulfilling and meaningful relationships, to help become a deeply spiritual person, help develop an equanimous mind, a compassionate heart, mindful living, which is the sacrament of the present moment, and an ever openness to others and especially to God. Meditation helps us to prepare the ground, and in that positive silence, solitude, and emptiness we will become open to God and the gifts of the Spirit. It is an openness that results in our journey in God and God's love.

There is far more to life than arising in the morning, going to work, having meals in between activities, returning home, watching television, sleeping, etc. If this is the case, then there is no difference between animals and human beings. I am not denying that life unfolds itself in the activities of the day-to-day life such as eating, working, cooking, gardening, doing laundry, sleeping, etc. The difference brought by daily practice of meditation, is that we constantly become aware that life not only flows in these moments, but also in the various activities of the day and that we are always connected with the source and center of life. When we realize this truth, then eating becomes a moment of celebration of life in the form of food, work becomes the channel for our creativity to flow, love becomes a moment of selfless giving to one another where passion and romance become part of true love. Soon our actions, decisions, intentions, and our relationships will be devoid of ego; every activity becomes a pure celebration of life and love.

Often people say, "If I do meditation, I will have to give up many pleasures of life. I cannot enjoy life, go to parties, join a dance, and take vacations..." The Jesus as presented in the gospels, celebrated life very much. Often, he compared the Reign of God to a wedding celebration. No one goes to a wedding celebration with a sad face or to be sad. There is so much joy, plenty of wine, music, and dance. The Pharisees even accused Jesus of being a glutton and a drunkard (Lk 7:34). Jesus often went to the home of those who invited him to dine. He reclined at the table and shared in their fellowship. He was happy to be in the company of people; he also welcomed little children and loved their company as well. He enjoyed the affection and love shown by Mary Magdalene. He often visited the home of Mary and Martha and shared meals with them. When Lazarus died he cried. Jesus had emotions and feelings. God is not a sad or a sadistic God, a life denying God. Quite the contrary, God is a life affirming God. It is not a sin or a crime to be cheerful. Where God is present, life is celebrated and where there is celebration of life, God is present.

Let us not forget that every morning and evening Jesus retreated to quiet places to pray. He chose early mornings and late evenings because those are the times when people would not disturb him. His day was sandwiched in between these two precious moments. He began the day with his Father and ended the day with his Father. In between he was always in the presence of his Father whether he preached, healed, walked, or chastised the Pharisees. Whatever he did, his Father's love flowed through his acts and words. This is the goal of spirituality. This is what meditation seeks to achieve for the believers. That is why meditation is not just a relaxation technique. It is not just to remain calm, peaceful, or more focused. Those are the by-products of meditation. The real goal of meditation is opening ourselves to the God-experience, to be in the presence of God waiting to be filled by God's presence and to let that presence flow through all of our daily activities. True meditation will never take us away from the joy of life. It will only bring us closer to life and to the real celebration of life. It is not a way to escape and run away from the activities of the day and night, but it is the way for these activities to flow from the source and the fountain that comes from within.

The truth is that meditation enables us to become aware of the difference between pleasure and happiness. Change in external life style is not the primary goal of meditation. God experience, awareness, being connected to the center of one's being, to live without the false ego, to be a better human being is the goal that we work towards. Absolutely for the person who meditates, there is nothing wrong with going to parties, enjoying a dance, relishing a healthy diet, taking a vacation, etc. The difference is that these activities do not qualify and determine the self, but it is the realized self that brings meaning to these activities. The person is totally and fully present to whatever the person does. They will not fret nor be sad or will their world suddenly come crashing down if they are not able to be present at any of these things. They know the difference between pleasure and happiness. They will be totally and fully present in each and every experience, whether joyful or sad, pleasant or unpleasant. They are fully present with the spirit of non-identification of the true self in their acts and knowing the impermanent and passing nature of their experiences. That is why they are totally present to each and every experience, whether joyful or sad, pleasant or unpleasant. They are able to remain equanimous. In the book of Job we read, "... the LORD gave, and the LORD has taken away; blessed be the name of the LORD" (Job 1:21). Buddha says, "In the face of failures and success, remain the same. For both are not permanent." Being equanimous does not mean that one does not enjoy life. Being equanimous is the true ability to enjoy inner freedom. They become free within. They are not psychologically attached either to the various experiences or to the sources of these experiences. The consequence of meditation practice is true freedom that results in the state of moment-to-moment awareness.

When one is really mindful, living from moment to moment, then one celebrates the miracle of life not only in the thick of a party, or while watching a great movie, but also in the loveliness and beauty of God's creation. We behold the miracle of life in the wonder of nature, in the penetrating rays of the sun, in the incredible beauty of the full moon and its light, in the twinkling stars in the blue sky, in the gentle falling rain, in the passing cool breeze, in the chirping of birds, in the fragrance of flowers, in the amazing majestic mountains and deep valleys, in the nourishing food, in the refreshing drink on a hot day. We come face to face with the miracle of life in the warmth and embrace of one's spouse, in the extended arms of a child, in the beauty of an affectionate kiss, in the spontaneous smile of a baby, in the marvel of relationships, in the mystery of love, in the sacredness of one's body, and in the beauty of sexual love in all of its intimacy. We witness life both in the joys and sorrows, in the age that is catching up, in the reality of pain and suffering, and in the truth of death and life after death.

Therefore, a person who lives with the light of awareness can never deny life. Meditation is life affirming. Meditation can only make us better people; more human, more loving, and more compassionate. That is the reason why even in old age, couples who have been meditating, find great meaning and joy in just being together, doing nothing. What happens if one of the spouses becomes quadriplegic? Does life come to an end? No. Their inner self, which sustains their love for one another, brings them closer to each other. The source of happiness and inner peace are within, not based on external things. It is from their own centers they reach out to others. Their relationship with each other becomes more meaningful precisely because it flows from their centers. Normally, people reach out to others to find happiness and joy. If this is the case, then all their life they will be moving from one relationship to another, falling in and out of love. Their life will be an endless search for people whom they think will bring them the nectar of life. The truth is no one can bring the nectar of life for us; it is already there within us. When we are in touch with this base, the fountain within us, then, it is this that flows out in all our relationships and all of our activities. It is in this way that relationships are meaningful. It is this that we affirm when we say so-and-so is peaceful, calm, loving, and compassionate.

The goal of meditation is to celebrate life, a celebration that flows from an intimate union with God. St. Paul said, "Rejoice in the Lord always; again I will say, Rejoice" (Phil 4:4). To be rejoicing at all times and in all circumstances with God and in God is the true meaning of spirituality. In this spiritual journey, meditation is only one way by which such a spirituality can be lived. There are other paths as well. It can be simple devotions, different styles of prayer, retreats, visits to churches, temples, mosques and other holy places, a nature walk, listening to music, visualizations, imagination, reflections, concentration techniques, etc. Each one has to find one's own path.

The challenge is to choose one's path and consistently walk on it. In this myriad of paths, daily practice of meditation will surely lead one to be constantly united with God, to discover genuine happiness, and to celebrate life in all its beauty.

After buying an ice cream, a man gave a twenty-dollar bill to a monk at the counter. When he asked for change, the monk told him, "Change must come from within."

Let genuine change come from within.

On a Practical Level

➢ *Learn a meditation practice and be faithful to daily meditation.*

➢ *Like keeping appointments with others, look at meditation in its initial stages as keeping an appointment with God.*

➢ *Have your own meditation space.*

➢ *Keep reading inspiring books on meditation.*

➢ *Attend meditation seminars and retreats.*

➢ *Join a meditation group that meets regularly.*

➢ *While driving, once in awhile it is good to listen to soft and melodious music or to an inspiring CD or tape.*

➢ *Learn to love silence.*

➢ *Once a week or once a month observe a day of complete silence.*

➢ *Retreat into your desert to be with God.*

➢ *Leisurely walk in the park.*

➤ *Stop and smell the fragrance of flowers and listen to the 'song of the birds.'*
➤ *Practice mindfulness by doing activities mindfully.*
➤ *Spend time tending to plants or arranging flowers.*
➤ *At times in prayer 'just be.'*

Oh God!

I am not asking for wisdom, knowledge or wealth.
All that I desire is to know you and love you.
My body, my mind, my heart, my soul,
    every cell in my body longs to experience you.
Help me to be united with you.
May I enjoy the communion that you and your Son
    experienced.
Give me the gift of experiencing you and just being with
    you.
Help me to go beyond words and concepts, just let me
    be with you.
Take away everything from me, but not your presence,
    I only need you.
"Like the deer that longs for running water so my soul is
    longing for you.
Like the watchman waiting for the daybreak so my soul
    is waiting for you, oh God."
Come take possession of me.
"My heart is restless until it rests in Thee oh God."
Let me taste your divine love.
Let me remain in your love, let me live in your love alone.

Meditation
which is being still and knowing God,
calls for a life of spiritual discipline.

Spiritual Discipline: To Become Like the Master

No one who puts his hand to the plow and looks back is fit for the kingdom of God.
—Lk 9:62

Every athlete exercises self-control in all things...
—1 Cor 9:25

A man consulted his doctor about his obesity. The doctor told him. "Walk five miles a day for a year. At the end of the year you will lose 50 lbs." The man followed the doctor's advice and walked five miles everyday from his home. At the end of the year he called his doctor and told him. "Doc, you are absolutely right. I have lost 50 lbs., but I have a new problem." The doctor asked him, "What's your new problem?" The man replied, "I have lost 50 lbs., but I am 1,825 miles away from home."

To be faithful consistently to a spiritual practice is one of the most difficult problems of spiritual life. Faithfulness to a spiritual practice only comes with spiritual discipline. We live in a restless culture where patience appears to have lost its meaning, discipline is frowned upon, and busyness is worshipped as a virtue. We seem to be always in a hurry. Life moves faster and faster, and we expect immediate solutions to our problems. To slow down is a modern sin. Look at a typical person: mobile phone in one hand, lap top computer bag across the shoulder, pager on a belt, a palm pilot to keep him on his busy schedule, wanting to know, "Will there be an internet connection on the flight, or in the coffee shop?" "Fast" has become the watchword: fast-food, fast music, instant coffee and drinks, fast conversations, fast track, and high speed internet connection. When the internet connection takes time, we become restless; at the traffic signal, if the person ahead of us is a bit slow to react to the changing signal, we become impatient; when traffic moves at a snail's pace we lose our "cool;" when the operator puts us on hold, we lose our temper.

We have grown physically stronger and the longevity of human life has increased, but have we grown spiritually? Has our spiritual consciousness developed? Are we experiencing higher forms of consciousness? Have we become better people? Is the world a better, safer place to live in now?

Like our external life that is controlled by high speed, so too, is our inner life, our spiritual life, and the continuous development of our consciousness determined by speed. We seem to have no time and patience for the development of the spirit. We want our spirituality on a fast track: Does this spirituality work? How long does it take? Yes, I want to experience God, I want peace, happiness, and joy but I want it now. This spiritual method is taking too much of our time. Is there another way, a quicker way to experience God? I have so many things to accomplish. I don't have time. I am a very busy person. Get on with religion. Don't waste my time. My time is precious.

We are constantly on the run. Where are we running to or from whom are we running? The greatest tragedy of the human person is, not wanting to pause and be still, to experience God. To pause and to be still requires spiritual discipline. A disciple, following the teachings and the spiritual practices of the master, eventually hopes to become like the master. Spiritual discipline is the process by which the disciple through a life of spiritual practices becomes like the master.

Great spiritual masters believed, lived, and taught that deep relationship with God is not possible without a life of spiritual discipline. Spiritual discipline is the backbone of the spiritual life. Before we proceed to understand some of the important features of spiritual discipline, let us look at the lives of Jesus and a few others, to understand the importance of spiritual discipline for spiritual growth.

Jesus of Nazareth

After his baptism, Jesus was lead by the Spirit of God into the desert. He was in the desert for forty days and nights spending time in prayer and fasting. In the desert he was tempted by the devil, and he did not give in to the devil or to his promises. In the desert, while it was a time of physical hardship for Jesus, it was also a time for spiritual growth.

The Physical Experience of Being in the Desert

The desert brings to our mind loneliness, fear, thirst, hunger, boredom, pain, frustration, depression, hardship, helplessness, hopelessness, insecurity, and dangers from wild animals and thieves. Having gone into the desert, Jesus, in spite of all the difficulties he faced in the desert, never gave up. The desert can really break a person, for in the desert we are reduced to nothing and nobody, and, we are forced to depend on God alone. It is a place of total trust and surrender to God. Life and forces in the desert can weaken or break the outer body, but not the inner spirit of a person whose life is centered in God. It was Jesus' inner strength, trust, and experience of God that enabled him not to succumb to the external dangers of being in the desert.

The Spiritual Experience of Being in the Desert

The people of Israel were in the desert for forty years. Those were years of spiritual experience and growth for them. Even after their freedom from slavery they wanted to return to Egypt. They constantly complained, grumbled, and even betrayed God. God literally had to break them down before he could re-build them as a nation and a people. It was in the desert that God established the Covenant with them, gave them the Ten Commandments, established different tribes, was with them through their battles, and eventually led them to the Promised Land. The desert was a time of letting go of the past and accepting God as the rock and foundation of their lives. It was a time of absolute trust and surrender to God. In the desert, the various experiences, though appearing to break them, in fact, strengthened them and made them rely on God alone. God destroyed their securities, broke them, molded them, and prepared them before they could reach the Promised Land. In all of these situations they were not alone; God was with them as "cloud by day and fire by night" (Ex 13:21-22).

Jesus, anointed and led by the Spirit into the desert, knew, that like his people and prophets in the Old Testament, he too, was called into the desert to be strengthened, to know and accept God's will and mission, and the means for achieving it, the way of suffering. The temptations that occupy an important place in the desert experience of Jesus, must be seen in the context of his baptism. At his baptism his Father declared, "... This is my beloved Son, with whom I am well pleased" (Mt 3:17). The core of the three temptations of Jesus was to deny his identity as the Son of God and to reject the way that God had chosen for him. Jesus rejects the devil and his promises and reaffirms his faith and trust in God as his Father, and commits himself to walk the path that God has chosen for him, knowing that God will always be with him. This was the inner struggle, the spiritual battle that Jesus experienced in the desert. From the desert, Jesus came out victorious over his own inner battles with the clarity of his mission, and a renewed commitment to his Father.

The Inner Resolve

In spite of the physical difficulties of being in the desert and the inner and the spiritual battles that he experienced, Jesus never gave up. At any time Jesus could have returned to the city, but he stayed on. He entered the desert with a strong resolve to see it through until the end. He trusted in God alone and knew that his trust would be vindicated by his Father. He was determined and focused; he prayed and fasted. He did not give up. The forces of nature or the devil did not weaken or break his determination.

Even during his public life, he withdrew into solitude and silence to be always centered in God. The devil that tempted him in the desert did not leave him once and for all; he returned to tempt him often, to lure him away from the cross and the path of suffering, but Jesus was always able to say "no" to the devil because his life was centered in God and God alone. It was his fidelity to his time with his Father in solitude and silence that made his inner resolve stronger. His determination to walk the path, maintain focus, and dedication to his mission, was the result of his fidelity to his time spent being with his Father in solitude.

He faced and accepted moments of loneliness, rejection, betrayal, suffering, and finally crucifixion. He was able to transform his suffering into a source of salvation for others. He found strength in fidelity to his moments of prayer, especially prayer in solitude that became his daily bread.

Gautama Buddha

Siddhartha Gautama was born in *Kapilavatthu*, India, near present day Nepal. His mother died when he was seven days old. Growing up in the palace he was exposed to all of the pleasures of life. His father made sure that he grew up not knowing ugliness, discomfort, sadness, suffering, or death. At night, when the prince was asleep, gardeners would remove all dead leaves from the palace gardens and whenever he went outside, going from the palace to the amusement park, the sick, the aged, and funeral processions were kept out of his path. At twenty-nine, he married Yasodhara and had a son, Rahula.

Once, on his way to see spring flowers in a nearby grove, for the first time in his life, he encountered suffering, old age, death, and a mendicant-monk. Seeing radiance on the face of the monk Siddhartha inquired who he was. His charioteer told him, "He is a monk who has renounced the world and its possessions in order to seek the true meaning of life." Siddhartha, then and there, knew what he wanted to do. He went home, bid farewell to his wife and his son, renounced his worldly life, cut off his royal turban and long hair, and went into the forest in search of truth, and the meaning of life.

It has been said that for six years, either on his own or with other seekers, he relentlessly searched for truth. He exposed himself to the great spiritual masters of his time, studying with them, doing yoga, and meditation hoping to find liberation. He fasted and did all the ascetical practices; the fasting and the practices were so rigorous that he became so weak and frail that when he felt his stomach it was his backbone that he was touching. He brought himself to the verge of death by starvation. Still he was not liberated.

Exhausted from starvation he laid under a tree. A woman saw him and brought him rice and milk.

Strengthened by the food, he recalled how as a child he felt sitting under a rose-apple tree and the great joy that he had experienced in his heart. In those few moments, without any effort, he had experienced spontaneous compassion and ecstasy. It was then that he decided, and was resolved, to sit beneath the Bodhi tree nearby and not to arise until he became enlightened. He said to himself, "Let only my skin, sinews, and bones remain, and let the flesh and blood in my body dry up; but not until I attain Supreme Enlightenment will I give up this meditation seat."

As he sat down with determination and resolve, *Mara* (death, his own dark self) under the guise of aversion, greed, lust, various delusions of the mind tried to tempt him. Siddhartha did not give in. With weapons of lightning, thunder, darkness, flood, fiery wind, trembling of the earth, and a tall tree burning in front of him *Mara* tried to scare him and break his resolve. Siddhartha sat unmoved and unaffected, with only his virtues to protect him. He remained determined and focused. At last he was enlightened and became the Buddha, the enlightened one.

The death of Siddhartha's mother and his encounter with old age, suffering, and death forced him to confront the emptiness and lack of meaning in life (the way he was living his life in the palace), which led him to set out to find the meaning of life. After trying various schools, he finally sat under the Bodhi tree with a determination not to get up until he was enlightened. Only with the bowl of rice and milk, Siddhartha would not have gotten his entire strength back as his body had almost collapsed due to starvation. Sitting under the Bodhi tree points to his dedication, determination, and his inner resolve to find the way out of suffering, the path to liberation.

Before Siddhartha became enlightened he always had alternatives: he could have stayed in the palace enjoying a life of material pleasures; he could have avoided an encounter with old age, sickness, suffering, and death; and he could have refused to face the reality of emptiness and the meaninglessness of his life. When the philosophies of various schools and his vigorous ascetical practices failed him, he could have given up his search and returned to his family. He did not. He continued his search even to the point of death. When everything seemed hopeless and his search brought him nowhere, he could have returned to the palace, but he did not. Though he was confronted with difficulties, and forces of nature brought against him by Mara to break his will and determination, he did not give up. He sat under the Bodhi tree focused and determined. His determination and dedication paid off.

Moses, Dogen, and Thomas Merton

In the Old Testament, Moses was raised as a Prince in Pharaoh's court in Egypt. He grew up with all the comforts of a Prince. When the Pharaoh came to know that he was a Jew, Moses could have denied it and continued to enjoy the life of a prince. Moses made a choice and faced the consequences of that choice, to live in the desert. For Moses who grew up in the palace, life in the desert was not easy. In the desert he experienced loneliness, fear, frustration, hunger, thirst, constant threats to his life, depression, and emptiness, but Moses did not give up. He continued to be in the desert.

In the desert he had let go of all of his securities and face his own vulnerabilities. In the desert he was reduced to nothingness. He had to let go of his dependence on everything and everyone and rely on God alone. In the desert he encountered his dark side and came face to face with his own shadow. He allowed the desert and its trials to transform him. Finally, it is in the desert that he encounters God who strengthens him, transforms him, and sends him on a new mission. In the desert he who experienced inner liberation becomes the liberator of his people. He did not run away from his emptiness and loneliness, but confronted them. Moses always had alternatives: he could have stayed in the palace, he could have ended his life in the desert, and after he met Reuel he could have stayed with him, but he made a choice and allowed the consequences of his choice to mold and transform him.

Dogen was born on January 2, 1200 C.E. in Kyoto, the capital of pre-modern Japan. He was born of influential parents. His father was assassinated when he was two years old and his mother died when he was seven years old. The masters of whichever monastery he entered died. He was constantly faced with the reality of death. Dogen, until he was enlightened, faced the emptiness and impermanence of everything.

Dogen, unable to find satisfactory answers to questions of emptiness and impermanence in Japan, undertook the difficult journey of going to China to find answers. When he went to China he was not allowed to enter the country so he stayed on a ship for three months. Finally, he was accepted by master Ju-ching and was enlightened. Dogen, like Buddha, never gave up his search. He could have enjoyed a successful political life, wealth, and great comforts, but instead chose to face the realities of emptiness and impermanence of everything. His determination, dedication, and inner resolve were not in vain; he became a great spiritual teacher.

Thomas Merton (1915-1968) lost his mother when he was six years old, his father when he was fifteen years old, and his brother during the war. He experimented with various pleasures of life and gave into vices to confront loneliness and emptiness, but as he did so, he became more and more miserable and empty. It was only in facing his emptiness and exploring its meaning that he found true meaning and purpose in his life, and in turn became a source of inspiration for many. Merton could have stayed in England; he could have continued to experiment with the vices and material pleasures of life; he could have given up his search when the Franciscans refused him; he could have left the monastery where he was often misunderstood, but Merton chose to stay in the monastery, and in choosing the path of meditation and embracing the life of a hermit, he found the meaning of life and God.

Growth in the spiritual life is not possible without desire, perseverance, determination, sacrifice, and focus. Jesus allowed himself to be led into the desert, faced the challenges of life in the desert, prayed, fasted, reaffirmed his trust and sonship in God, accepted the mission of the Father, and confronted the devil and his empty promises. Jesus came out of the desert victorious. Siddhartha, though reduced to the point of death did not give up his search to find the meaning in suffering. He continued to search until he was enlightened. He was determined and his determination paid off. Even after embarking on an inner journey Moses, Dogen, and Merton always had other alternatives. They stayed on track and remained focused. They faced various obstacles, difficulties, and challenges. Their determination led them to find true meaning in their life and they became an inspiration for many others. Jesus says, "... No one who puts his hand to the plow and looks back is fit for the kingdom of God" (Lk 9:62). Having embarked on a spiritual path there is no use looking back. St. Paul, writing to the Philippians says: "... but one thing I do, forgetting what lies behind and straining forward to what lies ahead, I press on toward the goal for the prize of the upward call of God in Christ Jesus" (Phil 3:13-14). Spiritual life calls for such a determination and focus in order to pursue the goal: a life of union with God.

In the letter to the Hebrews we read:

... and let us run with perseverance the race that is set before us, looking to Jesus the pioneer and perfecter of our faith... for what son is there whom his father does not discipline? ... For the moment all discipline seems painful rather than pleasant; later it yields the peaceful fruit of righteousness to those who have been trained by it (Heb: 12:1, 7, 11).

In the letter to the Corinthians he writes: "Do you not know that in a race all the runners compete, but only one receives the prize? So run that you may obtain it. Every athlete exercises self-control in all things..." (I Cor 9:24-25).

Discipline is the soil on which the athlete stands. Without discipline one cannot develop into a great athlete. As the author in his letter to The Hebrews writes, "For the moment all discipline seems painful rather than pleasant; later it yields the peaceful fruit of righteousness to those who have been trained by it" (Heb 12:11). The word discipline brings to mind unpleasantness, determination, dedication, sacrifice, and hard work. The truth is without discipline nothing worthwhile in life can be achieved. At that time, as the author says, discipline is not a cause for joy but later it bears fruit. This is true even with regard to our spiritual life.

Discipline, as noted at the beginning of this chapter, is the process by which the disciples following the teachings and practices of their traditions become like their master. This process involves: desire, focus, determination and perseverance, sacrifice, and consistent practice.

Desire

Spiritual life begins with a strong desire. Athletes have a dream, a desire, and a goal. They want to be *numero uno* in their field. It is this desire that drives them to be disciplined in body and mind and to be regular in their training. It was the desire to see Jesus that brought salvation to Zacchaeus and his household. It was Mary Magdalene's desire to know Jesus that brought out true love in her. It was the desire to learn from Jesus that was instrumental in bringing Joseph of Arimathea and Nicodemus close to him. Like the deer that longs for a running stream (Ps 42:1), like the sentry waiting for the day to break (Ps 130:6), and like the person immersed in water gasping for breath, so too our desire to walk the path of the inward journey, and to be with the indwelling presence of God, should be strong and real in us.

Focus

An athlete is clearly focused on the goal and strives to achieve that goal. When the mind is focused on the mission, then nothing will deter the person from achieving his goal. Jesus in his heart knew what was expected of him and the price he had to pay to accomplish the mission that God had chosen for him. He remained focused on his mission. Hence, he did not succumb to the temptations of the devil, his promises, or to what people wanted him to be. His words, acts, mission, and his life always remained focused on God and his given mission. Similarly, unless we remain focused on the spiritual path that we have chosen to walk, we will not make progress. Don't we all initially begin with tremendous enthusiasm and fervor, but along the way, for various and many reasons, our focus gets deviated? Rather than getting discouraged, refocus and start again.

Determination and Perseverance

A good athlete is strongly determined. Lack of determination is another weakness in our spiritual practice. In spite of facing various problems in the desert Jesus remained in the desert for forty days. Siddhartha sat under the Bodhi tree with the determination not to get up until he achieved enlightenment. Dogen was determined not to return to Japan until he reached enlightenment and so remained on the ship until he was accepted as a student by master Ju-ching. We expect to see results too soon. Dropping of negative mental states, the false self and then allow wholesome mental states to grow through God experience, calls for patience. In the process, along the way we will face innumerable difficulties and challenges. We need to be determined to overcome these obstacles and to persevere because in any spiritual practice, time and time again, we will go through stages of dullness, laziness, drowsiness, restlessness, worry, doubt, and boredom. We will experience the temptation of immediate gratification, suffer from spiritual procrastination and experience the "dark night of the soul." The secret is, no matter what we may go through, we must continue to persevere with our spiritual practice, with a strong spirit of determination.

Consistency in Practice

An athlete's practices are not conditioned by climatic conditions. It is not enough to practice sporadically. To be a good athlete climatic conditions are not excuses, but they become challenges to overcome. Similarly, we have to walk on our spiritual path each and every day. The gospels portray a Jesus who was in prayer and solitude everyday. The saying is true, "Daily practice matters," and so too, "Practice makes perfect."

Sacrifice

If an athlete wants to arise at five in the morning, he cannot be partying until late into the night. The body needs rest. Every choice comes with a decision to renounce something else. The choice to be a professional comes with the decision to renounce things that will prevent the athlete from achieving the goal. To carry the cross, Jesus had to say "no" to the promises of the devil and "no" to the expectations of the people. To be true to himself Moses had to leave the palace of the Pharaoh, accept the desert, and Siddhartha to find enlightenment he had to renounce the palace and become a mendicant-monk. Growing in relationship with God calls for sacrificing those things that will distract us from our spiritual practice and life.

Once there was a famous sculptor known for his life-sized statues of horses. They appeared so real. Someone asked him, "What is the secret behind your artistry?" The sculptor replied, "When I see a big rock I bring it to my workshop. For days I do not work on it. I just let it lie in the courtyard. Everyday, with total concentration, I keep looking at the rock from every angle. In the beginning I see nothing except a large piece of rock, but as days pass by slowly and faintly I see something in that huge rock. I become aware of something that is waiting to burst forth, it is just an outline, but it keeps growing stronger and stronger in my mind. Finally, when the outline becomes very clear, and I see a horse waiting to burst forth, it is then that I begin my work. With my chisel and mallet I chip away every bit of the rock that is not the horse. What finally remains is a horse."

The process of discipline chips away
at those elements that prevent the
true Christ nature from shining forth in us.

Oh God!

Somewhere along the way I give up my spiritual journey that I began with desire, fervor, and initial enthusiasm.

Lord, help me not to be discouraged.

Let me start again.

It doesn't matter how often I fall, may I rise and walk again on my spiritual path.

Almighty God, bless me with the grace of spiritual discipline.

Like Jesus, may I be determined and focused to walk the path.

Give me especially the grace of perseverance.

Through my spiritual discipline may I be graced with the joy of experiencing you my God and to share that joy with others.

To be still and to know God is to bear fruit in our life. Some of these fruit are: forgiveness, nonviolence, not causing hurt, pain, and suffering to others, spirit of sharing, spirit of gratitude, and not being jealous.

Forgiveness: The Path to Inner Freedom

Father, forgive them; for they know not what they do.
—Lk 23:34

If you want to see the heroic,
look at those who can love in return for hatred.
If you want to see the brave,
look for those who can forgive.
—Bhagavad Gita

In our life, often times, we either use or hear these phrases: "*It is human to err and divine to forgive*" and "*it is easy to forgive but difficult to forget.*" "*To forgive*" is different than "*to forget.*" Forgiveness is a virtue and a quality of the heart, "*to forget*" is an act of the memory. We need to develop the virtue of forgiveness, and in the process of continuous acts of forgiveness, the forgetting part will follow. What is forgiveness? How to forgive? Is there a limit to forgiveness? Should we continue to forgive to the extent that we allow ourselves to be humiliated and insulted again and again? What happens to people who choose to forgive and those who choose not to forgive? We shall attempt to understand the nature of forgiveness and the need to forgive by trying to answer some of the above questions. Let us begin by presenting some real events

119

from the lives of ordinary people that took courage to forgive.

Real Life Stories

While returning home from work one evening, Ron was robbed and shot to death by a drug addict. It was the most painful time in the life of Ron's parents and no human consolation would ever appease their pain and loss. For months they had to struggle with the loss of their only son, and feelings of anger and hatred were taking root in their hearts. However hard they tried, they could not come to terms with what had happened. One Sunday, during worship, they heard the words of Jesus, "Father, forgive them; for they know not what they do" (Lk 23:34). The words of Jesus disturbed them so much that for days and nights the words came back to haunt them. Finally, the parents decided to go and visit the man who had killed their son. It was the hardest decision they ever made in their life. The words of Jesus, "Father, forgive them; ..." filled their hearts, minds, and lips as they came into contact with the murderer of their only son. Ron's father slowly said, "We have forgiven you. Our son is dead and we will never have him again in this life. It has been very hard for us to forgive you, but today with God's grace we can say, "We forgive you." The man broke down and wept like a child. During all these months in prison, he had sufficient time to realize the heinous crime he had committed, and now with the words of forgiveness he knew that though he could not rewrite what had happened, he could fashion his future because of the forgiveness he had received. In fact that's what he did; he became an agent of peace and love.

Joe Mannath, in his book, *A Closer Look* shares the following true events:

> In Poona, India, I met a Belgian who shared with me a personal experience that is quite moving. In the Second World War, as we know, Belgium was overrun by Nazi Germany. During that occupation, a Nazi army tank had crushed his fourteen-year-old brother to death. Now that is certainly something any family would never forget. At the end of the war, churches in Belgium made the following announcement: The war has created many orphans in Germany, and these children will need families that would be willing to host them. Volunteers that were ready to welcome such needy German children were asked to give their names. The Belgian family went to the parish priest and offered to raise and care for the two German boys. The man that I met in Poona remembered the two boys who grew up with him on the family farm.

> Sheila Cassidy, an English doctor, committed the "crime" of treating a man who was chased by the police in Chile. For this she was arrested, taken to the police quarters, stripped, and tortured. Electrodes were connected to different parts of her body, and electric current was applied. Yet, during the torture, much to her own surprise she found herself praying, "Father, forgive them; they do not know what they are doing."

A Jewish woman in a Nazi concentration camp suffered great atrocities and witnessed human cruelty. Once she saw female Nazi guards waiting for a woman to give birth and then drowned the baby in cold water. She survived the camp and settled down in Germany. One day, she and a group of former inmates saw one of their old camp guards coming down the road with her child in a pram. The women, filled with the atrocious memories of the camp, rushed at the pram. The Jewish woman stopped them, saying: "We must not hurt the child. Otherwise, we will be like them." Someone turned to the woman and asked her, "How did you manage to preserve so much love in the midst of so much hatred?" Her touching reply was, "It is not that I have preserved love; the fact is that love has preserved me."

Compared to what these people suffered, our hurts, resentments, and bitterness may not be so dramatic. What is the nature of our hurts, pain, and resentments?

The Need to Forgive

It is true that all of us suffer from hurts. People, consciously or unconsciously have hurt us. The insensitive words and actions of family and friends; the betrayal by loved ones; breaking of trust, fidelity, and promise in relationships and business contracts; government policies; doctrines and dogmas; death of loved ones, etc. leave deep resentments in us. Children and parents hurt one another, spouses hurt each other, friends betray one another, employer and employees inflict much hurt and pain on each other.

All of us have been hurt, but only the degree and the intensity of hurt differ. If hurt is not properly handled, resentments take deep root in us. These deep rooted resentments are not like the lines drawn on the beach that are erased by the passing waves of the ocean, but they are like lines carved on solid rocks. They are too deep to be erased by the passing waves. The deeper these resentments are, the more harm they will cause to our bodies and minds.

The person who has caused us pain and sleepless nights may be away on a cruise or at a party having fun and continuing to enjoy life, not in the least aware of the pain they have caused another person, but we are the ones who suffer. Recently someone told me what happened at his office:

> Today, my supervisor who is also my friend hurt me very deeply by what he said to me. As I was leaving the office I was filled with anger and negative feelings towards him. Even after I reached home, I was restless. I could not relax with my kids or my wife, and as the evening progressed my feelings of anger kept rising in my heart. I had a drink and then one more drink to drown my anger, but it was of no use. I was restless and had a sleepless night. In the morning both my body and my mind were tired. I was sick. When I went to the office, my friend spoke and related to me as if nothing had happened. He said, "Last night I took my wife out for dinner and a movie. We enjoyed quality time together which we don't often have the chance to do." Then it struck me. He was the cause of my hurt; I had allowed his negative

actions to affect me, but it did not even bother him in the least; he had no concern whatsoever. He had a fabulous time with his wife, but for me, on the contrary, not only was my evening spoiled, I also made it miserable for my children and my wife as well.

The person who has caused the hurt oftentimes continues to live as if nothing has happened, but we are the ones who are afflicted and suffer. Reaction, rather than response to hurt, is what causes suffering in us.

We really need to forgive and learn to let go of hurt and resentment because if they remain in us they not only cause mental suffering, but also eventually can affect our health. We try to take good care of our bodies, but little do we realize that while we protect them from external dangers, we can allow many mental, psychological, and emotional irritants to affect our bodies and eventually cause harm to them. There is an intimate relationship between the mind and the body. The mind affects the body and the body affects the mind as well. Both the body and the mind harbor tensions or knots. Every mental knot has a corresponding physical, muscular knot and vice-versa. Mental disturbances create toxins in our body. These toxins get accumulated in different parts of the body, giving rise to diseases. This is because of the intimate relationship between body and mind. Psychic, emotional, and mental irritants keep us snarled up in emotional and physical bondage and manifest themselves as different types of diseases in our body. Most of our diseases are said to be psychosomatic.

Psychological studies have shown that clinging to past hurts has distinct emotional and physical consequences. Failure to let go of hurt and resentment, and, failure to forgive, can result in depression, anxiety, paranoia, narcissism, stress, tension, psychosomatic complications, heart disease, and also result in less resistance to physical illness. Constant remembrance of past hurts and hurtful situations will damage us both in body and in mind. Also, the more we harbor resentments, hatred, revenge, and anger, the more we give power to the other person to hurt and control us. Isn't the real enemy the one on whom we constantly project our own fears?

When we choose to forgive and share that forgiveness with the one who has caused us hurt, we are choosing to respond rather than to react. When we choose to respond, we accept the fact that we are hurt, that we are suffering. We understand what this hurt can do to our body and mind, and out of compassion we acknowledge that the other person is acting out of ignorance.

Forgiveness is the refusal to live in the past. It is a quality of living in the present moment. It is literally an act of dying to the past. It is an emphatic "no" to the past and to being a slave to the past. It realistically acknowledges that hurtful words and actions are only a memory without the reality of the present moment. It affirms that the past has importance only to the extent that it has brought us to the present moment and propels us forward to the future. Forgiveness is the decision to live in the sacrament of the present moment.

Forgiveness increases one's sense of compassion, love, and quality of relationships with others. To forgive is not to be naive. It is indeed the most courageous act. It paves the way for the renewal of wounded and broken relationships resulting in a rich, mental, emotional, physical, psychological, and spiritual life. In forgiveness one actualizes the biblical truth that one is the image and likeness of God, a spark of the divine, the eternal fire burning within us. God is forgiveness. When we choose to forgive we actualize the image and likeness of God in us. In letting go of hurt, bitterness, and resentment, we refuse to be prisoners within ourselves and we begin to savor the joy of inner freedom. When we are able to live from this freedom, we not only are healed, but we are also able to live from our true nature, the Christ nature within us.

Two ex-prisoners of war happened to meet each other. One asked the other, "Have you forgiven your captors?" The other replied, "No, never will I forgive them." The first one remarked, "Well then, they still have you in prison, don't they?" Are we free or are we still imprisoned?

Jesus and Forgiveness
It is important to forgive not only for a healthy, mental, emotional, and psychological well-being and

life, but also because, as St. John of the Cross says, holding onto past hurts and resentments will block the inflow of grace within us. The words in the Bible are very clear as to the necessity and the need to forgive:

> ➢ Our heavenly Father listens to our prayers only on the condition that we pray with a forgiving heart. "And whenever you stand praying, forgive, if you have anything against any one; so that your Father also who is in heaven may forgive you your trespasses" (Mk 11:25).
>
> ➢ God does not accept an offering when it is offered with an unforgiving heart. We might be happy to be fulfilling an obligation, but is our offering pleasing to God? "So if you are offering your gift at the altar, and there remember that your brother has something against you, leave your gift there before the altar and go; first be reconciled to your brother, and then come and offer your gift" (Mt 5:23-24).
>
> ➢ God forgives our sins to the extent that we are prepared to forgive those who have sinned against us. "For if you forgive men their trespasses, your heavenly Father also will forgive you; but if you do not forgive men their trespasses, neither will your Father forgive your trespasses" (Mt 6:14-15). Jesus concludes the parable of the Unforgiving Servant saying, "So also my heavenly Father will do to every one of you, if you do not forgive your brother from your heart" (Mt 18:35).

➤ Forgiveness is not being indifferent, but loving positively those who have hurt us and praying for their well-being. "But I say to you that hear, Love your enemies, do good to those who hate you, bless those who curse you, pray for those who abuse you" (Lk 6:27-28).

➤ Forgiveness is unlimited. It has nothing to do with numbers, it is *ad infinitum*. It reveals the quality and the attitude of the heart. "Then Peter came up and said to him, 'Lord, how often shall my brother sin against me, and I forgive him? As many as seven times?' Jesus said to him, 'I do not say to you seven times, but seventy times seven'" (Mt 18:21-22).

➤ Jesus not only preached, but also he showed in his own personal life that forgiveness is possible. As a master he demands the same from his disciples. "And Jesus said, 'Father, forgive them; for they know not what they do'" (Lk 23:34).

➤ Forgiveness is easy for the heart that is capable of love. "Therefore I tell you, her sins, which are many, are forgiven, for she loved much; but he who is forgiven little, loves little" (Lk 7:47).

➤ God has reconciled us and wants us to forgive others. "and be kind to one another, tenderhearted, forgiving one another, as God in Christ forgave you" (Eph 4:32).

God's living word invites us to a life of constant forgiveness. Without forgiveness love is incomplete. Our response to the offer of God's love, in and through the person of Christ, must arise from a heart that is free of hatred, anger, and resentments. Jesus reduces the entire law into two commandments: love of God and love of neighbor. Love of God results in love of neighbor and love of neighbor leads us to love of God. Neighbor, for Jesus, is not only fellow Israelites, but also non-Israelites and even those who do not like us, those who have hurt us deeply, and those who have betrayed us. "You have heard that it was said, 'You shall love your neighbor and hate your enemy.' But I say to you, Love your enemies and pray for those who persecute you" (Mt 5:43-44). For John, the disciple of Jesus, love is not possible when there are seeds of hatred present in our hearts. He says:

> He who says he is in the light and hates his brother is in the darkness still. He who loves his brother abides in the light, and in it there is no cause for stumbling. But he who hates his brother is in the darkness and walks in the darkness, and does not know where he is going, because the darkness has blinded his eyes" (1 Jn 2:9-11).

God is not an existence to be admired, but a presence to be seized and imitated. We are summoned to love others the way God loves us. If we accept the truth that we are created in the image and likeness of God, then living that image implies loving others as God loves us. The nature of God is love, and if God has breathed God's own nature into us, then aren't we centers of love? Is not love our true nature? Yes, our true nature is love and that is why the only commandment is, "Beloved, if God so loved us, we also ought to love one another" (1 Jn 4:11). "And this commandment we have from him, that he who loves God should love his brother also" (1 Jn 4:21). Only when we love others do we really come to know God: "... and he who loves is born of God and knows God. He who does not love does not know God; for God is love" (1 Jn 4:7-8). Loving others is living in God: "So we know and believe the love God has for us. God is love, and he who abides in love abides in God, and God abides in him" (1 Jn 4:16). Forgiveness is an important dimension of the biblical call to love. Hence, "If anyone says, 'I love God,' and hates his brother, he is a liar; for he who does not love his brother whom he has seen, cannot love God whom he has not seen" (1 Jn 4:20).

To be a disciple of Jesus is to follow the master. After washing the disciples' feet, Jesus tells them, "... Do you know what I have done to you? You call me Teacher and Lord; and you are right, for so I am. If I then, your Lord and Teacher, have washed your feet, you also ought to wash one another's feet. For I have given you an example, that you also should do as I have done to you" (Jn 13:12-15). In this event, it is good to remember that Jesus washes the feet of Judas too, knowing that soon he would betray him. Jesus even shares bread with him and lets him dip his bread in the cup. It is this Jesus that we are called to imitate, to share our love by an act of forgiveness even with those who have hurt us and betrayed us.

Forgiveness and Reconciliation

Forgiveness is unconditional and unconditional forgiveness never recalls the past. A strong desire to let go of resentments is inherent in the very nature of true forgiveness. As long as we hold onto resentments and hurts, true reconciliation is not possible. Genuine forgiveness leads to reconciliation. St. Paul writes to the Christian community at Corinth:

> Therefore, if any one is in Christ, he is a new creation; the old has passed away, behold, the new has come. All this is from God, who through Christ reconciled us to himself and gave us the ministry of reconciliation; that is, God was in Christ reconciling the world to himself, not counting their trespasses against them, and entrusting to us the message of reconciliation. So we are ambassadors for Christ, God making his appeal through us..." (2 Cor 5:17-20).

When God forgives us, God re-establishes the broken relationship with us. Along with God's forgiveness there is always the reconciliation. God does not just forgive, but renews the wounded relationship. The prodigal son was not only forgiven, but he was also given the opportunity to re-establish his relationship with his father and brother. Others who changed as a result of forgiveness are: Peter after his denial, Matthew, who left his old profession as tax collector, Zacchaeus who came down from the tree to host Jesus as a guest in his house. Their old life, in the words of St. Paul "had passed away and they were a new creation." Forgiveness of our brothers and sisters will be incomplete if it does not include the possibility of reconciliation. Forgiveness is willingness to be reconciled and to renew the broken relationship. Reconciliation is possible only when we are prepared to let go of past hurt and resentment.

When God forgives us our sins, God forgets the sins we have committed. For God, to forgive is to forget. God's forgiveness does not carry within it a record of the wrongs we have done. God's forgiveness is unconditional. When the prodigal son returns home, the father who is waiting for his son, does not wait to be told by his servants that his son has returned or wait for the knock on the door. Seeing his son walking down the road he runs to embrace him. The father does not wait for the son to finish his prepared speech, but calls for a celebration to begin. Once again he is accepted as his son. In the entire dialogue between the two, the father never asked about his life of dissipation, but accepted him back without the condition that he would not leave him again. For the father, the past did not exist, and the future was non-existent. Only the present was real; and the present reality was that his son had returned; he was lost but now found, he was dead but now alive.

After Jesus' resurrection, when he encountered Peter, who had denied him three times, Jesus did not say, "Peter, I loved you more than the others, I made you the head of my Church, yet you denied me. How can you do this to me?" All that Jesus asked Peter was, "... Simon, son of John, do you love me?..." (Jn 21:16).

From the moment that God forgives our sins, God has already forgotten them. Like the first rays of the sun that burn away the morning mist or when ashes are scattered in the wind, they cannot be gathered, so, too, God's forgiveness burns away our sins that can never be gathered again. When God forgives our sins, God forgets them. We are forgiven and we are called to forgive others. To share our forgiveness with others, includes our willingness to let go of our resentments. This is the most difficult part in the forgiveness process, for the human experience is just the contrary.

It is easy to forgive but very difficult to forget the harm that others have caused us. We are reminded about the hurt often. When we see them, hear about them or at the mention of their names or when we remember them, hurt and resentment fill our mind. Even after we have forgiven them and renewed our relationships with them, don't we, at the first opportunity bring up what they have done to us, especially when we are angry or upset? It is very difficult to let go of the memory of hurt feelings. First of all we should be honest and be realistic enough to accept that it is difficult to forget. Rather than concentrating on wanting to forget, focus on forgiveness. To forget is an act of the mind and it will take its own time. With repeated acts of forgiving, we will be able to let go of the stronghold that hurt has on our memory. Begin to love them; memory filled with resentments will become weak. Be healed; negative memory will lose its power over the human mind.

Does forgiveness mean that we keep running after the one who refuses to reconcile with us? Does it mean that we allow ourselves to be ill treated and insulted again and again? Does it mean that we allow the other person to treat us without respect? Jesus says:

> If your brother sins against you, go and tell him his fault, between you and him alone. If he listens to you, you have gained your brother. But if he does not listen, take one or two others along with you, that every word may be confirmed by the evidence of two or three witnesses. If he refuses to listen to them, tell it to the church; and if he refuses to listen even to the church, let him be to you as a Gentile and a tax collector (Mt 18:15-17).

Forgiveness does not condone the past. As said earlier, the past is useful in as much as it brings us to the present, and we can learn from the past. We should not be foolish and allow those things to happen to us repeatedly. We should take precaution and care not to expose ourselves to continuous hurt, pain, and suffering. Forgiveness implies being wise, not placing ourselves in similar situations that permit the other person to hurt us again. To forgive is not to be foolish. Recognize the condition that brought about your pain and suffering. Forgiveness is a call to let go of the hurt, resentment, pain, and suffering, but not to forget the conditions that brought about pain and suffering and not to continue exposing ourselves repeatedly to circumstances that may cause pain in the future.

In sharing our forgiveness we are essentially healed and our hearts are free from resentments, anger, bitterness, hatred, and negativities. We don't need to allow ourselves to be put in situations that may cause pain and suffering. We don't have to keep running after the other person when the other person does not desire to reconcile with us. On your side you have not burned the bridge. You are always ready and open to welcome the other person. Like the father in the story of the prodigal son, you are prepared and willing to establish the broken relationship with your estranged brother or sister. When Peter returned, he found Jesus was ready to accept him back. For various reasons the other person may not be prepared to be at peace with you; give him/her space and time, which will help heal all wounds. In your heart you have sincerely forgiven the other person, but you are also there to renew the broken relationship when the other person returns. Hence, a forgiving person is ready and prepared to welcome back his estranged children when they come back. When his or her spouse wants to start all over again with the resolve to be faithful, the forgiving person is ready and accepting. A forgiving person is ready to help the neighbor who wants to break down walls, and to open his heart one more time to the repentant friend who has betrayed him.

For a loving, forgiving, and compassionate person there are no real enemies. The only enemy is the enemy within. Through the grace of forgiveness such an enemy can be overcome. Forgive and experience the true joy of inner freedom.

On a Practical Level

In what concrete ways can we let go of anger, hatred, and vengeance? How can we drop feelings of hurt and resentment? How can we forgive? Listed below are some practical ways in which we can live a life of forgiveness:

➤ **Direct confrontation:** In some instances a direct encounter with the concerned person can result in reconciliation. Let the cards be laid on the table. Plain, straightforward talking gives an opportunity to clear misunderstandings, prejudices, and also gives a chance to listen to the other person and his/her viewpoint of the situation. It also helps to get resentment out of our system. Keeping a journal may be of help. Whatever means one may choose, the goal is to let go of resentments and to share peace and reconciliation with the concerned person.

➤ **Presence of a third person:** Talking it over in the presence of a third person who is neutral will function as a good catalyst; be impartial, and objective. In encounters and confrontations we tend to listen more to ourselves than the other person. Often, we are preoccupied with our own rebuttals and replies rather than wanting to listen to the other person. We may hear but not really listen; often, it is selective listening. The presence of a third person will be of great help to point out the dynamics and the nature of dialogue between the concerned parties. A third person may also help reveal the conscious and the unconscious motives and the presence of strong and selfish egos and pride that are within the individuals.

➤ **Realization out of compassion:** Ask yourself, "Why is the other person doing this to me?" People hurt us out of ignorance. Can Jesus hurt another person? A truly spiritual, enlightened, and a compassionate human being will not hurt another. Those who have realized their Christ nature continually live at a level of consciousness where they become compassion themselves. Their very nature is compassion and out of compassion they will not hurt others. When others hurt them, they will realize that they are acting out of ignorance. Jesus, prayed from the cross, "Father, forgive them; for they know not what they do" (Lk 23:34). They not only did not know what they were doing to the Son of God, but also to another human being.

➤ **Pray:** Jesus in the gospel of Luke says, "But I say to you that hear, Love your enemies, do good to those who hate you, bless those who curse you, pray for those who abuse you" (Lk 6:27-28). Jesus invites us to love them, to do good to them, to bless them, and to pray for them. This is literally overcoming evil with good. It is easy to start with prayer and eventually the other three will follow in due time. When we pray for the one who has hurt us, we are in fact going beyond feelings of hurt and resentment and wanting only the best for them from God. When we pray for those who have hurt us, let our prayer be positive. There is a famous Buddhist prayer that expresses this positive aspect of prayer very well. *"May this person be happy* today. *May no harm or evil come upon this person today. May this person be filled with happiness, joy, peace, and love. May this person's life be filled with prosperity and blessings. In the face of inevitable problems, may this person have the strength, wisdom, and courage to overcome them."* When we pray positively for those who have hurt us, we not only invoke God's blessings upon them, but also our own negative attitudes towards them slowly undergoes a transformation. This prayer will create positive energy within us, which in turn can change our attitudes towards them, and it can eventually affect even those who have hurt us.

➤ **As God's Will:** In faith look at every act of hurt, resentment, and injustice as part of God's plan of salvation. Jesus' own crucifixion was God's plan for him. Matthew in his gospel often quotes the words of Jesus, "That the Scriptures may be fulfilled." To accept everything that happens in our life as part of God's plan is to surrender our life into God's hands. Our knowledge is only of the present. God's infinite wisdom knows what is good for us not just for this day, but also for our entire future.

➤ **Look at the crucifix:** Did Jesus deserve death by crucifixion? For no fault of his own he was put to death. He accepted the cross, the crucifixion, and his painful death as his Father's will. Compared to what he accepted in perfect obedience, what are our hurts, resentments, bitterness, and reactions to injustices? "… If any man would come after me, let him deny himself and take up his cross and follow me"

(Mk 8:34). At times, crosses we are called upon to carry come with feelings of hurt, resentment, and anger at the injustices that others have inflicted on us.

➤ **Singular Act of Grace:** Look at the figure of Jesus on the crucifix and ask him to give you the grace to forgive those who have hurt you. With grace nothing is impossible. In prayer surrender the feelings of hurt, anger, hatred, and resentment to God and ask God to bless you with the grace of forgiveness. Sometimes, it is possible to let go of the hurt in a moment of deep prayer and experience peace. Then it becomes possible to quit having a pity-party for yourself.

➤ **Realize:** Always remember that when we pray we are asking God to forgive our sins as we forgive those who have sinned against us. We have seen that God will not listen to a prayer that arises from a heart that is filled with hatred and anger. We pray, "Father forgive our sins…" Whenever we turn to God asking for forgiveness, God forgives us. We also experience being forgiven by others. God expects us to share our forgiveness with others. Let the chain of forgiveness continue. Let it not end with us. We have been forgiven; it is a gift. The gift entails a mission, a call to forgive others.

➤ **Meditate:** When we die nothing stays with us in the grave. If we look in the casket we will not find our hurts, bitterness, and resentments. We leave all those feelings behind. If they do not come with us, why should we carry them around while we are alive? Drop them. Only the fruit of our actions will come with us. One such fruit is forgiveness.

➢ **Revisit:** In deep prayer go back to the situation that was hurtful, not alone, but with God. With the loving and strengthening presence of God relive those moments. What really went wrong? Often we blame the other person totally but we forget that in some ways we too are responsible for the breakdown of a particular relationship. Be honest. What can we learn from it? Ask for the grace to let go and experience the grace of healing. Surrender it to God. In prayer realize that bottling up hurts and resentments is not good for our physical, spiritual, mental, and psychological well-being.

➢ **Repeated Acts of Forgiveness:** Forgive, continue to forgive and keep on forgiving. Every time memories of hurt come into our minds let us forgive and let go. In repeated acts, forgiveness becomes easy and one fine day we will experience total forgiveness.

➢ **Count your blessings:** Life comes to us with its variety of experiences: love, joy, happiness, beauty, sadness, pain, suffering, and injustices. Compared to the blessings we have received, the injustices are minimal. Unfortunately, our memory often recalls only the few unpleasant experiences and not the many acts of love and kindness that we constantly receive from others. We suffer by remembering only the unpleasant experiences. Compared to poverty, misery, violence, denial of basic rights, which thousands of our brothers and sisters go through everyday, what is the nature of our hurts? Literally everyday we need to count our blessings; often we take for granted the blessings and the benefits that we experience daily in our life. At the end of the day, if we look back upon the life that we have lived, we would realize that we received more blessings than hurts, more love than hate, more pleasure than pain, more joy than suffering. Count your blessings and not your hurts.

A famous musician's wife complained to him one day about how badly an acquaintance had treated her. She thought he would become angry, and use his considerable influence to humiliate that individual. Instead, this is what he suggested to his wife: Go out, and do the nicest thing you can think of for someone else. That will restore the balance in the universe

—Joe Mannath, A Closer Look

Forgiveness is a decision to do good.
Overcome evil with good.

Oh God!

You have known me even before I was conceived in my
*   mother's womb.*

You have carved my name on the palm of your hand.

Even if my mother forgets me, you will never forget me.

You died for my sins, so that I could be free.

My God, you have loved me and no one can ever love
*   me the way that you love me.*

Yet, by my sins I have wounded you and caused you
*   pain. You not only forgave me, but also give me the*
*   possibility to reconcile with you.*

Never have you turned your face away from me.

When forgiving me you do not remember my past.

Lord! I am forgiven; help me to forgive as you do.

Let forgiveness flow through me.

May I not hold onto hurt and resentments.

Help me to let go of them and be healed.

Help me not only to forgive, but also to be reconciled.

May I forgive not seven times, but seventy times seven.

Evil and Suffering: Learning to Trust in God

Man therefore is divided in himself.
As a result, the whole life of men,
both individual and social,
shows itself to be a struggle,
and a dramatic one, between good and evil,
between light and darkness.
—Church in the Modern World 13

For I do not do the good I want,
but the evil I do not want is what I do.
—Rom 7:19

The Reality of Evil and Suffering

It is very painful and difficult to express in words the terrible devastation that was caused by the tsunamis that hit Asia, the hurricane Katrina in the U.S. and the earthquake in Pakistan. The reality that we witnessed in these countries was far more real, traumatic, and painful than the perception of it from the news media.

On December 26, 2004 and on the following days the entire world witnessed the fury of nature on the lives and the habitat of people of Southeast Asia. Thousands of lives were lost; entire families wiped out and in some cases only one member in the family survived. Babies were orphaned; properties were destroyed. Thick concrete blocks were thrown about, and iron rods were broken or bent. Trawlers and fishing boats were destroyed or washed miles inland. There was rubble everywhere. Corpses lay decomposing, and mutilated. There were mass burials. The smell of disinfectant was in the air. People were in fear of epidemics breaking out. One couldn't escape the stench of death. Frightened and insecure people were left homeless, along with many children. Volunteers, both religious and secular were trying to help people. The faces of people showed the blank look of shock and fear. Fishermen were afraid to venture back into the sea. Hospitals were overflowing with the sick. There was a conundrum of suffering, pain, frustration, helplessness, hopelessness, and sorrow.

Even before the world could come to terms with the havoc and the loss of lives caused by the tsunamis we are witnessing the pain, suffering, and sorrow to thousands of people caused by the hurricane Katrina in New Orleans and the earthquake in Pakistan. Confronted with such realities one is left with too many questions and very few answers.

Against the onslaught of natural calamities, the pain and suffering that they bring to the victims and to people all over the world, we begin to wonder who is responsible for such terrible tragedies. Often, when we are confronted with pain and suffering as a result of natural calamities and human tragedies, we begin to wonder whether God, as the creator of this universe, is responsible for such calamities? Why is there evil, pain, and suffering in this world? Who and what are really responsible for the presence of evil and suffering in the world? Is God the sole culprit? Is the world evil by itself? Couldn't God have created a better world? Are our selfish acts responsible for evil and suffering in the world? Is evil and suffering the way of the world, the law of life? Can we ever justify evil and suffering? Are there answers to these difficult questions?

We can sincerely attempt various religious, philosophical, and theological answers to explain the reality of evil, pain, and suffering. However hard we may try to understand, the "why" of evil will always remain a mystery. In spite of various answers, evil is a reality in the world. In India, the country where I grew up, the spiritual masters often narrate the story about the boy and the crocodile as a response to the question about the presence of evil.

A crocodile trapped inside a net said to the boy, "Would you please release me?" The boy replied, "If I release you, you will grab me." The crocodile said, "I will not do that to my benefactor and helper." The boy tried to release the crocodile and as he did so, the crocodile grabbed him. The boy said, "So this is what I get for my good action." But the crocodile responded, "Well, this is the way of the world, this is the law of life." The boy disputed this and asked a bird sitting on a branch, "Bird, is what the crocodile saying correct?" The bird replied, "The crocodile is right. Listen to my own experience. I was coming home one day with food for my fledglings. Imagine my horror at seeing a snake devouring my young ones, one after another. I kept screaming and shouting, but it was useless. The crocodile is right. This is the way of the world, and this is the law of life."

The boy asked for one more chance. There was an old horse on the bank of the river. "Is the crocodile right?" asked the boy. The horse replied, "The crocodile is right. Look at me. I've worked and slaved for my master all of my life. Now that I am old and useless, he has turned me loose, and here I am wandering in the forest waiting for a wild animal to put my life to an end. The crocodile is right. This is the law of the world, and the law of life."

The boy continued to beg to be given one more chance. The crocodile agreed. The boy saw a rabbit passing by, and he said, "Rabbit, is the crocodile right?" The rabbit asked the crocodile, "Did you say that?" The crocodile said, "Yes, I did." The rabbit said, "Well, we've got to discuss this, but how can we discuss it when you've got that boy in your mouth? Release him; he has to take part in the discussion, and if he tries to escape, with one slash of your tail you could kill him." "Fair enough," said the crocodile, and he released him. The moment the boy was released, the rabbit said to the boy, "Run!" As the boy ran the rabbit said to the boy, "Why don't you bring your villagers here, kill the crocodile, and have a banquet?" That's exactly what the boy did. The villagers came and killed the crocodile. The boy's dog came along also. When the dog saw the rabbit, the dog gave a chase, caught hold of the rabbit and throttled him. By the time the boy arrived at the scene, it was too late. As he watched the rabbit die, he asked himself, "Was the crocodile right? Is this the way of the world, is this the law of life?"

Evil, pain, and suffering are realities that we find in the universe, around us, and in us. We are born into a world where the presence of evil is a reality. By my birth I have not brought evil into this world. Evil pre-existed my birth. Though I am not responsible for its pre-existence, I am born into this world, which is not only good, but also contains the presence of evil. Hence, rather than looking at evil, pain, and suffering from a philosophical or theological point of view, I feel an attempt to understand the meaning of evil, pain, and suffering from a spiritual point of view will not only help me to cope with the reality of evil, but also enable me to find meaning in life in spite of evil, pain, and suffering. Such an attempt was made by Job in the Old Testament, who from an intellectual point of view (as his friends suggested), was never quite able to understand why he was made to suffer, but when he surrendered his intellectual query in faith to God and trusted in God, only then was he was able to find meaning in life in spite of evil, pain, and suffering.

Where is God?

Evil struck Job. He lost all of his property, his children died, and he suffered from a terrible illness. His wife told him to curse God for the sufferings that God had brought upon him, but Job rebuked her saying that God was not responsible for the misfortune that had befallen him. His friends using the law of retribution, tried to justify his suffering. Job, always just and righteous in the eyes of God, rejected their arguments. For Job, his suffering was neither due to his past, nor to the sins of his parents, nor even to personal wrong doings, nor was it a call from God to repentance. Job, a man of integrity and righteousness, felt that his suffering was unjustified, and thus he rejected the arguments of his friends. Finally he gave in to the temptation that he had been fighting against all along. The tragedies and the calamities that Job had experienced broke down his world and caused a lack of meaning in his life. He no longer saw order and harmony in the universe, or meaning in his own faith. He began to blame God for his suffering and demanded that God respond to him personally. In his dialogues with God and in the revelation of God's own omniscient and almighty power, Job was able to change his attitude and began to trust in God. Out of this trust he began to realize that even the just may suffer and what was called for was not the "why" of suffering but "faithfulness" to God, God's power, and God's presence. Gradually a matured faith emerged in Job, a faith that held on to God, a faith that submitted everything, even his sufferings, to God.

God made Job realize that evil and suffering can also befall the righteous, just as riches can be appropriated through evil and wicked means. Riches and wealth need not always be seen as a sign of blessing from God; nor should sufferings and calamities be seen as signs of a curse, punishment, or alienation from God. In surrendering to God, Job saw a new dimension of faith, a faith that enabled him to see harmony in the universe as a mystery to be esteemed rather than a theory to be mastered or questioned. He did accept that he would never understand the inherent laws of the universe. Hence, the external circumstances that govern the cosmos were of no more importance to him. Good can exist along with evil. Job, the just and the innocent, was struck by evil and experienced suffering, and he never understood the reason for his suffering. Because of his renewed faith in God's providence and presence, he was able to look at evil and suffering from a totally different perspective, the perspective of faith. From the moment he trusted God, he began to see harmony in nature whereas before he only saw deficiency. This basic trust in God and his shift in worldview enabled him to continue to live in spite of his experience of evil and suffering.

Haven't we, as human beings, experienced and continue to experience evil, pain, and suffering in our lives? Are we not exposed to terrible heart wrenching situations? Have we not come face to face with total destruction, both in our personal life, in the lives of our dear and near ones, the society, and the world at large? The loss of human lives and property caused by natural calamities, disasters, poverty, misery, and injustice leave us questioning. All forms of exploitation, manipulation, death of a loved one, betrayal, divorce, business and financial loss, sickness, discrimination in all forms, terrorism and anti-terrorism, dictatorship, religious fundamentalism and fanaticism, war, violence, lack of respect for life in all stages... compel us to question the apparent meaninglessness of life, of this world, and, shakes our own faith. Our inability to grasp the meaning of life in the face of evil, pain, and suffering leads us to a situation of frustration, helplessness, hopelessness, even to the point of losing faith in God. Confronted with the realities of evil and suffering, don't we, like Job question our own worldviews, beliefs, value systems, the order and harmony in the universe, and even our strong faith in a personal God? Philosophically, theologically we try to understand and grasp the meaning of such situations, but when our paradigm shifts, we are left with nothing but our faith, and at times, even such a faith seems to give way.

Trying to justify evil and suffering by having recourse to various arguments will be of no help. That's what the friends of Job did, to justify his suffering by looking for external reasons. Will it be of any help to tell your child that her pain and suffering are due to the laws of retribution? In the face of natural calamities or personal sufferings, mere intellectual answers will not help us to find meaning in life or in the operations of the universe. The "why" of evil and suffering will always remain beyond human comprehension. When faced with such moments, it is not an intellectual play of words that will help us, but faith in God and knowing that God is not the cause of evil and suffering, and that God is present with us and in us in our suffering. One of the victims of the tsunami who had lost everything and everyone in his family, said to me, "I have lost everything, but not God. I have no one to hold onto now but God alone. God is my rock and refuge. God is not only my creator but also my savior." This is strong faith, a faith that tries to find meaning in life even in the midst of terrible evil and suffering.

In the face of evil, pain, and suffering it is not, "Why me, Lord?" but rather, "What is your will Lord?" Like Job, our attitude should be, "But he knows the way that I take; when he has tried me, I shall come forth as gold" (Job 23:10). In faith, we ought to feel the presence of God, not only when the going is good, but also when evil, pain, and suffering befall us. This may be a stumbling block to some and a folly to others, but for those who believe in God, they can become opportunities to experience the presence and closeness of God. We find God not when we question or challenge God in the face of evil and suffering, but rather when we submit to God's will, power, presence, and knowledge.

The purpose and goal of our life is to enter into communion with God. Knowledge of God in the Bible is to grow into a personal relationship with God. This involves an intimacy and a sense of belonging that can only be experienced in the context of this special intimate relationship with God. Total surrender to God and acceptance of God's will, no matter what happens in our life, is possible only in the context of this close relationship. Being in relationship with God, enables us to find further meaning in life in spite of evil around us and in us. We may not have an intellectual grasp of the way God functions and governs the universe or allows the presence of evil in the world, but trust in

God born out of a personal relationship, will not only help us to cope with suffering, but also to continue to find hope and purpose in life not withstanding evil and suffering. It is here that Job stands out as a wonderful model for us. Job feared the Lord and turned away from evil. He was blameless and upright in the eyes of God, but Job, as I pointed out earlier, identified material possessions and wealth with the blessings of God. When material wealth was taken away, he perceived evil and suffering as a curse from God. Only when he was finally open to God's presence and justice as the center of his life and of the cosmos, that God could transform him.

Jesus often speaks about his communion with his Father. He says, "I and the Father are one" (Jn 10:30). Jesus experienced this intimate union. In the garden of Gethsemane, pain, agony, and loneliness made Jesus plead with his Father, "... My Father, if it be possible, let this cup pass from me; nevertheless, not as I will, but as thou wilt" (Mt 26:39). Again on the cross, in excruciating pain he cried out, "... My God, my God, why hast thou forsaken me?" (Mt 27:46). Jesus felt the presence of evil around him; he was in terrible pain, and was abandoned by his disciples. As a human being, out of this pain and suffering, he cries out to his Father, but still in the same breath he says, "... 'It is finished'; ..." (Jn 19:30). And the gospel goes on to point out that Jesus bowed his head and gave up his spirit. In Jesus' pain and suffering on the cross, in that loneliness, his Father was with him. Even in those terrible moments, Jesus who throughout his life experienced union with his Father, continued to feel the closeness and the presence of his Father even on the cross. Jesus was not alone on the cross. God did not take away his suffering, but God was with him to strengthen him in his suffering. For Jesus, "I and the Father are one" (Jn 10:30) was not only real in his public life or in moments of personal prayer, but also on the cross. His Father was with him right until the end. God was waiting to be united with Jesus on the cross. It would not be an exaggeration to say that his heavenly Father was closest to Jesus on the cross.

God, as our loving Father, does not intend evil and suffering for us, but when evil and suffering do befall us, God is right there with us. God's presence is more real to us than our own shadows. God is always with us, even in our pain and suffering. We are never alone. We all remember the concluding part of *The Footprints: During your times of trial and suffering, when you see only one set of footprints, it was then that I carried you.*

God is more alive in our tragedies than our glories. Isn't the saying true that God writes straight on crooked lines? Jesus suffered, but his suffering became a redemptive blessing for us. It is through the cross that Jesus saved us from our sins. St. Paul's words on the paradox of the cross are marvelous. He writes:

> For the word of the cross is folly to those who are perishing, but to us who are being saved it is the power of God. For it is written, "I will destroy the wisdom of the wise, and the cleverness of the clever I will thwart." ... Has

not God made foolish the wisdom of the world? ... For Jews demand signs and Greeks seek wisdom, but we preach Christ crucified, a stumbling block to Jews and folly to Gentiles, ... For the foolishness of God is wiser than men, and the weakness of God is stronger than men (1Cor 1:18-25).

Great eloquent words on the paradox of the cross! Good Friday is transformed into an Easter. The tragedy of Good Friday becomes the source of new life for us: sadness gives way to joy, death to life, sin to grace, slavery to freedom, and weakness to strength. Through Christ's suffering God has reconciled us. St. Paul captures it so beautifully when he says, *"By his wounds we have been healed."*

Through our suffering we are not only united with Christ's suffering, but also when we trust and surrender our suffering to God, God uses our suffering for our own good and the good of others. Suffering and pain have become a wake-up call in the lives of many. Broken relationships have been renewed and estranged families reunited around the bed of a dying person. Did we not witness the entire world coming together, wanting to do something for the victims of the tsunami, the hurricanes, and the earthquake? Some, in faith, see suffering and pain as vocation. A priest friend shared with me the following incident:

Once I was called to a hospital to visit a friend who was in terrible pain. While I was driving to the hospital, I was pondering how I would find the appropriate words that would help her to accept her suffering. When I met her, she soon understood my predicament and in spite of her pain, with a smile on her face, she said: Does not the gospel point out various ways of following and imitating Christ? Some imitate Jesus the Good Shepherd, others imitate Jesus the preacher, still others imitate Jesus the contemplative, and a few others imitate Jesus the servant. Often, we forget there is also the suffering and crucified Jesus to be imitated and followed. This is my Jesus. I see it as a vocation given to me by God, 'Come, follow me.' I am summoned to follow him through my suffering and pain.

To be able to accept pain and suffering, as this woman did, requires tremendous courage and faith. Ironically, he who went to console his friend, learned from her example, and returned with a much stronger faith.

Subjective Evil

So far we are trying to understand objective evil and suffering. As an objective evil it has an autonomous existence. It exits prior to one's personal acts. Because we are born into a world that has a sinful situation, as human beings we are continually influenced by evil. As per the doctrine of original sin, we who have been wounded and broken are inclined to evil and sin. Doesn't St. Paul write, "I do not understand my own actions. For I do not do what I want, but I do the very thing I hate... So then it is no longer I that do it, but sin which dwells within me... For I do not do the good I want, but the evil I do not want is what I do. Now if I do what I do not want, it is no longer I that do it, but sin which dwells within me" (Rom 7:15-20)? We are born into a world of sin and evil which, by its very nature, has the power to alienate us from ourselves, others, nature, and God. Because we are born into this already existing condition of the world, suffering, calamities, tragedies, and pain will always be a part of human life. This is the *objective evil* over which we do not have control.

Besides the objective evil there is also the *subjective/personal evil.* It is a rupture of relationships at all levels. It is a refusal to love, to be loved, and to relate to others in a positive, life affirming/giving way. It is anti-life. It affects one's willingness to assume responsibility for others. The root cause of subjective/personal evil is one's selfishness that arises from one's own heart. While objective evil pre-exists, and as a people we have no control over it, over subjective evil, we do have control.

There is an intrinsic relationship between objective and subjective evils. We are social beings. As social beings through our social relationships with others, we create and maintain social structures. Thus, the quality of a society is determined by the quality of relationships between members in that society. Therefore, decisions and acts, executed in a relational context have consequences that affect the members of the society. Hence, my personal evil, born out of my own selfishness, will not only bring pain and suffering to others in the context of relationships, but also contribute to the creation of unjust social structures. Every act of an individual affects the society, either for good or bad. My personal evil arising from my selfishness not only contaminates the social structures, but also continues to perpetuate evil in the world. We are not only born into this social structure that has already been contaminated by the pre-existing evil, but we also bring about more evil in this world with personal acts of evil.

Personal freedom, decisions, and actions are inseparably social and affect the social structures for good or bad. Thus, by our selfish decisions and actions, however personal they are, we add to the already existing evil in the world. The universe becomes more and more contaminated by our personal evil acts. Each one of us, by our personal acts of evil, is responsible for the accumulation of more evil in the world. As a human person I do have control over subjective/personal evil caused by my decisions and acts. Whether or not to be evil or to do evil is under my control. With my choices, decisions, and actions I can either be a perpetuator of evil or I can reduce the condition of evil in the world. Acts of subjective evil only add to the already existing objective evil in the world. Besides, acts arising out of our evil nature: anger, violence, murder, rape, stealing, lying, greed, jealousy, envy, resentment, mindless words, actions, gossip, etc. only bring suffering and pain to others.

With grace, discipline, and strong determination, it is possible to let the good take control of the evil in us. Constantly we need to be aware not only of our actions, but also our intentions, attitudes, thoughts, words, desires, and cravings. The macrocosm is a reflection of the microcosm. What is out there is a reflection of what is going on within me. Evil originates in the heart. An unclean heart is the seat of evil. Murder is the result of anger in my heart, stealing is the result of greed and craving in my heart. Evil grows from within. Subjective evil is in our control. The solution is within. Evil structures will not be converted until we who are responsible for them are converted and experience conversion within.

Our unkind and mindless words and deeds cause tremendous pain and suffering to others, but we are often insensitive to the pain and suffering of others until we experience them in our own lives or in the lives of our beloved ones. In this context the following Buddhist story makes tremendous sense: Qui Wong took great pride in his hunting skills. Once, while hunting, he spotted a deer with its young one tagging along. The hunter aimed at the fawn. The doe from the corner of her eye saw the hunter and before she could warn her young one, an arrow pierced her fawn. As the fawn lay bleeding to death, the doe stood behind a tree with tears running down her eyes. There was so much pain in those tears, but the hunter was so happy and proud of his shot and of the hunt. One day, while out hunting again, he took along with him his young son and left him under a tree as he went further into the forest to hunt. As he was waiting for his prey, he heard the rustle of leaves in a nearby bush, took a good aim at the spot and released the arrow in the direction of the bush. He heard a shrill cry from the bush, but the hunter was happy that his shot did not miss the intended target. He went happily to gather his prey, but when he came to the spot, to his shock and sorrow he saw his only son bleeding to death. He had killed his own son. He was inconsolable and his heart was filled with pain and sorrow. For the first time, he understood the meaning of pain and suffering, and as he suffered, he not only understood his own pain and suffering, but also that of the doe.

Should we wait to experience pain and suffering in our lives and in the lives of dear ones to realize that our unkind and mindless words and actions can cause tremendous pain and suffering to others? Every action produces an effect. Our wicked thoughts (mental), mindless words (vocal), and insensitive and selfish actions (physical) always produce pain and suffering in others; they never return to us empty-handed.

The golden rule is: *Do unto others what you want them to do unto you* (cf. Mt 7:12). *(Do not do unto others what you do not want them to do unto you).* No one wants to experience pain and suffering. The secret is being mindful of our thoughts, intentions, words, and actions. It is to plunge into that pause for that split second before we speak and act, to know for ourselves, whether our words and actions will hurt others. Don Rinaldi, the third successor of Don Bosco would say, "Think well of all, speak well of all, and do good to all." If only seeds of goodness, kindness, love, and compassion are nurtured in our hearts, then somewhere in the world someone is taking the first step to reduce the presence of evil and suffering in the world.

Pain

On one hand we should strive not to bring pain and suffering into the lives of others, but on the other, as human beings, we do experience pain no matter where it comes from. As human beings we are constantly exposed to different kinds and degrees of pain both in our minds and bodies. We suffer from physical, emotional, spiritual, and psychological pain. We do not wish to have pain, but it does happen and it is real. How do we deal with pain? First of all we must accept that pain is real. Do not continue to live in an unrealistic world that denies pain in our existence. Conversations, socials, magazines, T.V. programs, etc. constantly deny pain. We tend to pretend that pain does not exist. Are we not constantly on the run to protect ourselves from our own fears of facing pain? The truth is that, evil, pain, and physical sufferings are realities that cannot be denied. They in fact do exist. They are real. The process of aging, sickness, and death bring pain and suffering. Pain is an intrinsic part of being born with a mind-body; the question is, how do we deal with pain?

We are in the habit of using various strategies to deal with pain. *Are we in the denial world,* consciously denying its real existence and living in a makeshift world trying to fool ourselves that it does not exist? We hope and fool ourselves that it is not real and that it does not exist, that it is only in our imagination, but however hard we may try, pain does not go away. It is there in our body-mind. It is real. *Are we in the wishful world,* wishing that it will go away? Pain calls for our attention and now and then we give it a bit of our attention, hoping that pain will go away, but it does not. *Are we in the world of symptoms alone?* When pain cries out for our attention, the only attention we give is the medical attention. At the first sight of pain, we rush to take pain reducers. The pain goes away, but soon it returns; again we run to the world of medicine and this cycle carries on. *Are we in the real world?* In this world we accept that pain is real and that we need to take proper medicine to be relieved of the pain. Pain can be so intense, throbbing, aching, irritating, and devastating. We should take care of pain, but treating pain with painkillers is just dealing with the symptoms. Symptoms are only the tip of the iceberg. Only when we stop fighting with pain, when we are with it, open to it, and present to it, then are we able to grasp the true nature of pain. What is needed is an awareness of pain, an awareness that will reveal the true nature of pain itself. Pain is a sensation in constant flux; it keeps moving and changing. Sensations arise and fall, they are not permanent, but are constantly changing and dissolving. This is the true nature of pain.

Openness to pain will reveal an underlying reason that is causing this pain. The real problem is not pain, but what is causing the pain. Often, pain, sickness, and suffering are signs and symptoms of other deep-rooted problems. Besides treating them, we can look deeply and root out those causes that have given rise to sickness, pain, and suffering. Most of our psychosomatic sicknesses are only symptoms of deep-rooted causes. Let us say, for example, I suffer from headaches. The first time I have an attack of a headache, I take some medicine. The pain goes away. When the attack comes around a second time, I take more medicine and soon the intake of medicine keeps increasing, but the headache continues to reoccur again and again. The pain resulting from constant headaches asks me to look for a cause that is in my mind-body. Pain tells me that something is wrong with me (besides physical causes and chemical imbalances); maybe I need to change my food or sleeping habits or take control of my stress, constant worry, and anxiety. Awareness and staying with the pain will take us to the level of causes. By opening to the true nature of pain we become free within. The experience of being present to what is happening in mind and body is one of the best gifts that we can give to ourselves.

On a Practical Level

> ➤ **Accept** the truth that evil and good coexist. Just as evil and good are found together in the universe, so too, seeds of evil and good coexist in each one of us. While the human nature is good, it is also inclined to evil. We are capable of doing both good and evil and the battle between the good and the evil will always go on. Happiness and pain are inseparable. Both are experiences of being human. The source that gives rise to happiness is the same

source from which suffering and sorrow arises as well. Through conscious effort, permit the good to overcome the evil. If we are capable of doing good, we are also capable of doing evil; and equally if we are capable of doing evil, we are also capable of doing good. We have a choice to become saints or devils. It all depends on what we choose to manifest.

➢ ***Empower*** yourself by choosing to do good acts. Evil is the absence of good, just as darkness is the absence of light. To dispel darkness, one need not fight against or be overwhelmed by darkness. However old the darkness is, all that one needs to do is turn on the light and darkness disappears. So too, we need to allow the good in us to shine forth. Every time we choose the good and do good acts we are empowering ourselves. Every "no" to evil is a reaffirmation of our own inner strength to fight against evil. The old habit of being evil can only be broken by forming a good habit, and by repeatedly doing good acts, the new habit of doing good will be strengthened.

➢ ***Surrender*** to God. Just like Job finally surrendered to God, learn to surrender your experience of evil and pain to God. Learn to trust in God. Remember that it is not a question of "Why?" Lord but "What, Lord?" In faith believe that God is not the architect of the evil that has befallen you, but God is with you in your sufferings and pain. God is not a bystander or spectator. God is involved in every aspect of your life.

➢ ***Realize*** that our personal acts of evil, mindless words, and insensitive acts bring suffering and pain into the lives of others. Let us remember that by our personal acts of evil we not only maintain the structure of evil in the world, but also increase the presence of evil in the world. Remember the golden rule: *"Do not do unto others what you do not want them to do unto you."*

➢ **Trust** in God. When we surrender our pain and suffering to God, God is able to bring good out of evil. In our suffering and pain we not only identify with Jesus who suffered, but just as Jesus' suffering became redemptive, so too, God can make use of our suffering to bring about good both for us and others. When we let God into our suffering, suffering begins to have an inner value.

➢ **Pain and suffering** bring to our awareness the preciousness of life. They increase our love and we reach out to others in compassion. Suffering and pain increases our own inner understanding and strength. They bring out the best in us. They make us become more human. Jesus was moved with love and compassion when he saw people who were lonely (the lepers, sinners, outcasts), people who suffered (the sick, the widow of Naim, the sisters of Lazarus), people that were hungry, and people who were like sheep without a shepherd. In John's passion narrative, when the guards came to arrest Jesus, he tells them, "... so, if you seek me, let these men go" (Jn 18: 8). In the midst of his own suffering Jesus thinks of others, that they should not suffer on account of him. Again when one of the disciples of Jesus struck the slave of the high priest and cut off his right ear, Jesus healed him (Lk 22:49-50). In spite of his own agony, Jesus not only sympathizes with the slave but also reaches out to him and brings him healing. Once we can understand our own pain and suffering, we will not only be open to the pain and sufferings of others, but we will also have a desire to reach out to those who suffer.

➢ *Walk on a spiritual path.* People who are spiritual and are faithful to a spiritual practice will not harm or bring about suffering and pain in the lives of others. They act out of compassion and reach out to others. Their very core become centers of compassion. Living from this center, they will not hurt others. The secret is to find out our own spiritual path and walk consistently on it.

➢ *Pain can really be hurtful,* but it can also be a source of blessing as well. It all depends how we look at it. Besides, when we approach pain with awareness and mindfulness, we not only open ourselves to the true nature of pain, but pain can also teach us that it is only an effect of a deeper cause. The effect changes when the cause is transformed.

➢ *Reflect on Scripture.* The Bible is filled with the promises of God. Continue to read and reflect on God's comforting and reassuring words:

"... I have called you by name, you are
mine..." (Is 43:1)
"When you pass through the waters I will be
with you; ..." (Is 43:2)

*"... when you walk through fire you shall
        not be burned, ..." (Is 43:2)*

*"... I have graven you on the palms of my
        hands; ..." (Is 49:16)*

*"... Even if these may forget, yet I will not
        forget you." (Is 49:15)*

"... I am with you always, ..." (Mt 28:20)

---

*A man approached Mulla Nasrudin to seek help to
overcome the problem of gossiping. Nasrudin sent him to
the market to buy a chicken and told him to remove all
the feathers of the chicken before he brought it to him.
When he returned with the chicken, Nasrudin told him
to go back and bring all the feathers. The man laughed
and said, "Nasrudin, you must be mad, how can one
gather those feathers now? The wind would have blown
them off in all different directions. It is impossible to
gather them back." Nasrudin told him, "The same is true
with gossip, words that are once uttered cannot be
taken back or unkind acts that are done will not only
have their desired results, but their effects can never be
recalled."*

---

*Words and acts can either bring happiness or
pain and suffering to others.*

Oh God!

I constantly suffer from the battle between good and evil in me.

My spirit is willing, but the flesh is weak.

I want to do good, but I end up doing evil.

May your grace help me to empower the good in me.

With your Spirit may I realize that all that I need to do is to surrender my experience of evil, pain, and suffering to you alone.

When I am in pain and suffering I know that you are with me.

I believe that your presence in me is more real than my own shadows.

May I not increase the presence of evil that already exists in the world.

By my mindless words and insensitive acts let me not bring pain and suffering to others.

Fill my heart with love and understanding knowing that just as pain and suffering may hurt me, so too my words and acts bring pain and suffering to others.

Help me not to use mindless and insensitive words that bring pain to others.

May your Spirit of compassion help me to practice the golden rule: "Do unto to others what you want them to do unto you."

Nonviolence: The Healing Power of Peace

Peace I leave with you; my peace I give to you;
not as the world gives do I give to you.
—Jn 14:27
Blessed are the peacemakers,
for they shall be called sons of God.
—Mt 5:9

The Reality of Violence

The twentieth century was the bloodiest century in our recorded history. We experienced world wars that included Pearl Harbor, Hiroshima/Nagasaki, and genocide. We saw civil rights and freedom struggles in various countries. In this century we have the events of 09/11, increasing terrorism worldwide, and now the war against terrorism. We have had kidnapping of innocent persons for ransom, being held hostage resulting at times in murder. Wars and battles are continually being fought. Armaments, war, and violence determine international relationships. Nations witness violence within their borders, all in the name of caste, creed, color, culture, and clan.

Violence is not only in the streets but also at the societal and family levels: homicides, killings, shootouts, domestic violence, etc. Innocent lives are being lost, families are broken, children are orphaned, and properties are destroyed. Violence destroys relationships, shattering the physical and the emotional lives of individuals. Violence leaves everyone in a state of shock, grief, frustration, and anger. Are we not living in a culture of violence, mutually destroying each other?

Violence is becoming an addiction. Violence dominates conversations, comic books, cartoons, television ads, serials, movies, and even the spirit of nationalism. The best strategy for and against war determines the election of country's leaders. Many tend to believe in the saving power of violence and the myth of *"redemptive violence."* Can violence overcome violence? Are we not getting more and more trapped into the vicious cycle of violence? Violence begets more violence. Why do so many continue to live with the false belief that violence and war can bring peace? It is said that animals hunt for their prey only when they are hungry, but only the human beings are capable of hunting for pleasure alone. Animals, among the same species, do not kill each other, but the intelligent human species kill one another.

There is a beautiful Zen story about the man who was riding a horse at a breakneck speed. His friend asked him where he was going? He said, "How do I know? Ask the horse." That has become our situation with regard to violence. Violence has overtaken us, and we are becoming victims of our own violence. We have lost control of violence in our world and society.

Day after day, hearing stories of violence throughout the world, some even begin to wonder whether peace is ever possible. Let us be realistic.

While it is true that violence is on the rise, it is also equally true that there are individuals, groups, political leaders, lawmakers, social activists, and religious people who not only condemn violence in every form, but also work for peace. Though they are small in number, their voices still can be heard. Through signature campaigns, fasts, manifestations, and through various programs and activities, they try to create awareness against the culture of violence. There is a tremendous consciousness against having recourse to violence as the only solution to global, national, societal, and personal problems. There are people who believe that peace need not be just a utopian concept, but that peace is possible and that relationships at all levels can be governed by peace.

Microcosm and Macrocosm

In this chapter, my focus is not on external activities, structures, policies, and decisions that would yield peace at the global, national, and societal levels, but to explore a little deeper and to reflect on "Peace I leave with you; my peace I give to you; not as the world gives do I give to you..." (Jn 14:27). The world tries to give external peace through violence, fear-punishment, and policies, etc. but; at the most, external forces can create an external social order where there is peaceful co-existence. Can peaceful co-existence be tantamount to an experience of peace? Is it not true that external peace should be a continuum of the experience of inner peace? The use of various intoxicants and drugs can result in an altered state of consciousness, but it is only a temporary feeling, a feeling that depends on external objects, *but peace is a state of being, a way of life.* It is this inner peace that Jesus was talking about. It is this peace that is capable of healing, both the oppressor and the oppressed. Peace is a commitment to a spirituality of nonviolence.

J. Krishnamurthi is correct when he said that the macrocosm is a reflection of the microcosm. What goes on at the global, national, societal, and family levels are a reflection of what goes on within each individual. Are there not dark tendencies, both conscious and unconscious, negative impulses within our own psyche, that give rise to various forms of violence that manifest itself in our thoughts, words, actions, decisions, choices, values, and relationships? Are there not seeds of violence in our minds that we constantly water and nurture? Reflecting on 09/11, Pope John Paul II in his General Audience on September 12th said, "Yesterday was a dark day in the history of humanity, a terrible affront to human dignity... How is it possible to commit acts of such savage cruelty? The human heart has depths from which schemes of unheard-of ferocity sometimes emerge, capable of destroying in a moment the normal daily life of a people..." All of us carry within ourselves the seeds of unheard–of ferocity. From time to time, don't we all experience grave deviations from what we are meant to be? Often, don't we escape from our own dark and hidden shades, various types of sickness, blindness, and insanity? Don't we suffer from anomalies, peacelessness, forms of aggression, and violence in our own selves?

Before analyzing structural violence let us honestly look into our own selves and our relationships. Are they not governed by selfishness, violence, and peacelessness? An objective and unbiased self-inquiry would reveal that very often we consider the other as a threat not only to our life and to our existence, but also to our success and well-being. Is it not true that a strong distrust of the other, refusal to share power, love for materialism, success, achievements and accomplishments, superiority complex, covetousness, jealousy, envy, aggression, etc. continue to create and maintain a cult of violence? No wonder the human person was defined as "a wolf unto others."

A society is formed and sustained by relationships between human persons. The individual contributes to the collective structure and is in turn maintained by the collective structure as lived out in human relationships. In this network of human relationships, the external social structure reflects the inner psychological structure of the individuals. A relationship is like a mirror. It reflects our own true nature. If there is anger, hatred, jealousy, envy, mistrust, strong animosity, brutality, antagonism, or emotional negative feelings, it is these that will be reflected in our relationships and form the foundation of our society. If the mind is filled with compassion, forgiveness, understanding, sensitivity, caring, sharing, love, purity, innocence, peace, goodness, self-control, faithfulness, kindness, patience, joy, gentleness, and nonviolence, it is these qualities that will be reflected in the choice of our values, decisions, intentions, words, deeds, actions, and our relationships. Unless and until each one of us becomes the center of peace and non-violence, real peace at large is not possible. Gandhi beautifully said that one must become the change that one wants to see in others.

We are both individually and collectively responsible for every war because of our own selfishness, ego, intolerance, biases, prejudices, and aggressiveness in our own lives. The greatest challenge to violence is to experience peace and non-violence within ourselves. Wonderful policies can be drafted, structural changes can come into existence through new legislation; but no real peace is possible until each one of us experiences the therapeutic power of inner peace and nonviolence within ourselves.

Spirituality of Nonviolence

Like Jesus, with God's grace it is possible for each one of us to live from our own true and original nature, a nature that emanates only love, forgiveness, and compassion. Life is a harmonious blend of the outer and the inner. The inner expresses itself in the outer and the outer reflects the inner. To realize this, we need to live our life from the very deepest core of our existence.

Often, most of us are alienated from our own true self. In this culture that seeks and glorifies false self-identity we have forgotten the spiritual dimension of our own true self. What is the real nature of the self? When the self drops all its false pretensions, in its ultimate reality, it is nothing but an image and likeness of God, a spark of the divine, a pure existence, an uncontaminated consciousness without any dichotomy; it is pure awareness. A child's consciousness is pure, but as the child grows, his consciousness becomes defined and redefined by the contents from the outside. As a mirror that reflects anything that is held in front of it, likewise a consciousness reflects what is contained within it. The structure of the consciousness is defined by its contents, the contents that have been placed there by us. The contents of our consciousness are reflected in our relationships. In other words, our relationship is characterized by the contents of our consciousness. Thus, if our consciousness contains seeds of negativity, then negativity will be reflected in our relationships. If our consciousness contains seeds of wholeness, then our relationships will reflect this wholeness and goodness. If we take seriously the biblical truth that each one of us is created in the image and likeness of God, then the spark of the divine is the very nature of our consciousness. If only we can allow this spark to take root within us! It might be difficult, but it is possible. It may be a life long journey, but a journey begins with a step. Let us try to understand this important truth by looking at the lives of some other people who have allowed peace and nonviolence to become the very nature of their consciousness.

Jesus

The gospels repeatedly affirm the truth that Jesus was the Son of God. Jesus lived to his fundamental truth that he was the Son of God. His words and actions reflected this fundamental truth. His ministry was a continuation of his union with his father. He said, "Do you not believe that I am in the Father and the Father in me? The words that I say to you I do not speak on my own authority; but the Father who dwells in me does his works" (Jn 14:10). Like his father who is defined as love, Jesus, too, chose the path of love, compassion, and nonviolence. At his baptism, the Spirit of love and peace descended upon him. In the desert, each temptation was a call to deny his own true identity. Throughout his public life until he died on the cross, he never succumbed to the desire of his people to lead them against the Romans, or to come down from the cross. If Jesus had done so, that would have been the very denial of his identity. Jesus lived and died by love, reconciliation, peace, forgiveness, and nonviolence. It is these that formed the content and the structure of his consciousness.

His words reflected his consciousness: "... Put your sword back into its place; for all who take the sword will perish by the sword" (Mt 26:52). Referring to forgiveness he says, "... I do not say to you seven times, but seventy times seven" (Mt 18:22). Jesus points out that it is not only killing that is sinful but even anger is equally if not more sinful: "But I say to you that every one who is angry with his brother shall be liable to judgment; ..." (Mt 5:22). It is not hatred but love that directs all of our relationships: "But I say to you that hear, Love your enemies, do good to those who hate you, bless those who curse you, pray for those who abuse you. To him who strikes you on the cheek, offer the other also; and from him who takes away your cloak do not withhold your coat as well" (Lk: 6:27-29). In the same passage he goes on to say, "But love your enemies, and do good, and lend, expecting nothing in return; and your reward will be great, and you will be sons of the Most High; for he is kind to the ungrateful and the selfish. Be merciful, even as your Father is merciful" (Lk 6:35-36).

Not only his words, but also his actions reveal love as the core of his very being. Jesus' love led him to the cross. God did not choose a violent method for Jesus to overcome evil in the world. Jesus lived and died the suffering servant:

> He was oppressed, and he was afflicted, yet he opened not his mouth; like a lamb that is led to the slaughter, and like a sheep that before its shearers is dumb, so he opened not his mouth. By oppression and judgment he was taken away; and as for his generation, who considered that he was cut off out of the land of the living, stricken for the transgression of my people? And they made his grave with the wicked and with a rich man in his death, although he had done no violence, and there was no deceit in his mouth (Is 53:7-9).

And again "a bruised reed he will not break, and a dimly burning wick he will not quench; ..." (Is 42:3).

Jesus would have been long forgotten had he died using violence. On that Good Friday, violence destroyed his human body, but not his inner spirit. It was this spirit that enabled him to reach out to his oppressors and say, "Father, forgive them; for they know not what they do" (Lk 23:34). It is from the cross, by his nonviolence and forgiving love, that Jesus overcomes the vicious cycle of violence and destroys the myth of redemptive violence. The oppressed, without any power, becomes more powerful than the oppressor and often becomes an agent for change in the oppressor. A nonviolent act breaks the chain of violence. Though he was exposed to every form of violence, he remained nonviolent and remained true to love. According to the Christian tradition, "by his wounds we are healed." By his death, reconciliation and forgiveness have been made possible. Jesus' option for the path of love brought him to a violent death, but it was precisely on the cross that love was at its sublime best. To all people of good will, the call from the cross is to live by our original nature, a nature that reflects God alone.

Gautama Buddha, Gandhi, Dr. M.L. King, Jr.

No matter what he encountered in his life, Gautama Buddha was well-known for his peace, compassion, and non-violence. A man who doubted the possibility of such a state, decided to put Buddha to a test. This man went to Buddha's place and, it has been said, that for three days he was rude, cruel, and also found fault with everything that the Buddha had taught.

Much to his surprise, his continual verbal abuse did not get the Buddha to react even once to this man. On the contrary, each time the Buddha responded with love and kindness. Unable to elicit a negative response from the Buddha, the man finally asked the Buddha, "How can you be so peaceful and kind when I have only been very cruel, unkind, and negative towards you?" The Buddha replied, "If someone offers you a gift, and you do not accept that gift, to whom does the gift belong?" The man received his answer.

If someone offers us gifts of hatred, cruelty, anger, foul language, or hostility and we do not accept them, then they remain with the giver. Why should we become upset, irritated, or angry regarding something that does not belong to us? The Buddha, through the practice of meditation, became a compassionate person. Living and being faithful to a spiritual path can enable us to develop a compassionate, nonviolent heart, and a healthy state of mind. This is what the Buddhists call the "Buddha nature" that is within each of us. Let the dormant Buddha nature that is within us become awake.

Mahatma Gandhi's philosophy of life was guided by *ahmisa* (non-violence) and *Satyagraha* (search for truth). *Ahmisa* not only characterized his personal life, but through a life of ahimsa, Gandhi proved to show to the world that the impossible can truly become possible. Gandhi and his followers' non-violence played an important role to bring an end to the British rule in India. It was Gandhi who said that he did not hate the British but what they did in India. He even went to the extent of saying that if the British were not prepared to leave India as friends, then he was prepared to let them rule him. It is no wonder after its independence; India opted to become part of the British Commonwealth. Gandhi strongly believed that the chain of violence couldn't be broken unless one experiences the power of nonviolence and peace within oneself. External change can only begin with internal change. For Gandhi: *Become the change.* For him, one's inner experience of peace and nonviolence flows into one's relationships with others and all that one does. What appeared to be Gandhi's weakness in the eyes of many, became the source of strength and inspiration for so many, and continues to inspire many people. Gandhi fought against evil without becoming evil.

Dr. Martin Luther King, Jr. was very much inspired by the *ahimsa* of Gandhi. He believed that the path of peace and nonviolence does not immediately change the heart of the oppressor; but like Gandhi, he believed that first it will bring change within the person who opts for the path of nonviolence. In confronting violence they are able to connect to their own inner source and strength. It is in opting for the path of nonviolence that we will pave the way for reconciliation and an end to violence. The objective is not to change the enemy, but to change oneself. When one is connected to the center of one's being, then all their activities will flow from that center. Dr. King assured his oppressors that no matter what they do to his people, they would continue to receive only love in return. This is the spirituality of peace and nonviolence.

If Gandhi, Francis of Assisi, or Dr. Martin Luther King, Jr. sought revenge on those who had injured them, would they continue to inspire the world as they do? If Teresa of Avila, Therese of Lisieux, Mother Teresa, Oscar Romero, had been women and men of violence, would they have touched our hearts so deeply as they do?

Nonviolent Resistance

On the one hand, for some, redemptive violence is justified. Their thinking and response seems to be trapped in the vicious cycle of violence. On the other hand, there are others who believe in choosing the path of absolute pacifism, practicing absolute non-resistance. In between there is the group that believes in just war. For them not all wars are justified, but some wars can be justified on certain grounds. It is not a question of disarmament, but what weapons can be justified in a war. Is there really no other way out? Are we asked to turn the left cheek when one strikes us on the right cheek? Are we asked literally to give away the tunic as well when one asks for the cloak? Does Jesus really advocate absolute non-resistance? Suppose your spouse is abused or attacked, can you be non-resisting, thinking that resistance would amount to violence? If you see a physically handicapped person insulted, can you just keep quiet? If you witness acts of injustice right in front of your eyes, can you be non-resistant? Should you be non-resistant at all times?

The Jesus of the gospels clearly states an emphatic "no" to violence in any form, but at the same time the gospels have revealed Jesus as one who has resisted injustices. Jesus did resist. When he was struck on the face, he asked the man who struck him, "... If I have spoken wrongly, bear witness to the wrong; but if I have spoken rightly, why do you strike me" (Jn 18:23)? When the temple was desecrated, he was upset and turned the tables upside down. He defended the rights of the poor, the oppressed and the outcasts against the might of the Pharisees and the Scribes. He was a voice for the voiceless. He fought against both the religious and the social aristocracy. Although in his resistance there was no trace of violence, Jesus never taught people to be passive in the face of injustice. To be meek and humble of heart does not mean to accept every form of oppression and injustice that is meted out to you. The three sayings of Jesus about turning one's cheek, giving one's tunic as well, and walking the extra mile should not be taken in a negative sense of weakness and a call for non-resistance. The real interpretation of these sayings of Jesus is an invitation for us to resist injustice, but in a nonviolent manner.

Gandhi, following the spirit of the beatitudes, called for civil disobedience resulting in the famous salt march in a nonviolent behavior. It is possible to respond to injustices in a non-violent manner. The way of Jesus, Buddha, Gandhi, and Dr. Martin Luther King, Jr. is a call to transcend both passivity and violence. It is no wonder that Gandhi said, "The first principle of nonviolent action is that of noncooperation with everything humiliating." The difference between the approach of violence and nonviolent resistance is the means used to overcome injustice.

For Thomas Merton nonviolence is inseparable from prayer. It is not a strategy to be adopted, a technique to be followed, even a specific choice to be made in life. Nonviolence is life. It is a vision of life, a spirituality. Any resistance stems from this spirituality.

One evening, while sitting by their camp fire, a wise old Indian chief told his grandson about a great battle that was going on inside himself, and also, inside his grandson. He said, 'My son, a battle rages within each of us; it is between two wolves. One is evil; anger, envy, sorrow, regret, greed, arrogance, self-pity, guilt, resentment, inferiority, lies, false pride, superiority, and ego. While the other is good; joy, peace, love, hope, patience, serenity, humility, kindness, empathy, generosity, truth, compassion, and faith." "Which wolf wins?" asked the grandson. The old Indian Chief simply replied, "The one I feed."

Which one do you feed?

On a Practical Level

> ➤ Be mindful of your attitudes, words, and actions. Stop and think before you react in a violent way. Rather than reacting, try to act and respond in a proactive way.

> ➤ Live from the center of your being which is peace and nonviolence. Walk a spiritual path. Be consistent with your spiritual practice. Do meditation, yoga, go for walks, listen to soft, melodious, healing, and soothing music.

> ➤ Make an effort to remove all channels of violent input from your life: audio and video materials that provoke violence; avoid talks, ideologies and people who inspire violence; keep away from people who are negative.

> ➤ Pray your scriptures.

> ➤ Read biographies of Gandhi, Dr. Martin Luther King, Jr., Oscar Romero, Mother Teresa...

> ➤ Reflect on the 'Prayer of Peace' of St. Francis of Assisi.

> ➤ Decide to be an instrument of peace. Be involved in peace. Remember that nonviolence is not just the absence of violence. Be proactive.

> ➤ Reject excessive activity. Try not to be caught in the labyrinth of accomplishments and success. Where there is competitiveness there is aggressiveness.

> ➤ Constantly become aware of your own aggressiveness and peacelessness as it manifests itself in your words, actions, decisions, choice of values, and your relationships.

> ➤ Try not to be aggressive while driving.
> ➤ Practice silence.
> ➤ Avoid consumerism, love for power, and the desire to dominate. These are forms of violence. Learn to let go.
> ➤ Avoid being narrow-minded and intolerant to the views and ideas of others. Be open to the views of others. No one has the monopoly on truth. Many interpretations are possible. Do not force your views on others. People have a right to be different.
> ➤ Listen and overcome the tendency to interrupt someone who is talking. Learn to listen.
> ➤ Cultivate the habit of speaking only constructive words that will inspire hope and confidence.
> ➤ Decide to protect life wherever possible.

Oh God!

May I realize that nonviolence is not just the absence of violence.

May I constantly be aware that the external structure of my society is qualified by the inner psychological structure of my own being.

May I behold the pure light of my consciousness.

I am your own image and likeness.

I am spark of you, O divine.

May that spark keep shining brighter and brighter.

May I be peace, light, and love.

May my words, actions, and relationships reflect you O divine light.

May I not fall into the temptation of redemptive violence.
By transforming myself may I bring the transformation
*   that I wish to see in others and the society.*
May I be an instrument to break the cycle of violence by
*   my own compassion and nonviolence.*
In the face of injustice may I have the courage to
*   practice nonviolent resistance.*
May I be peace.

Gratitude: The Feeling of the Heart

It is never good to let the thought of
good things done pass away.
Of things not good, it is good to rid
your memory that very day.

Kindness shown by those who
weigh not what the return may be;
when you ponder right its merit,
it is vaster than the sea.
—Tiruvalluvar

A French lady was on a cruise ship. It was early in the morning and as she stood on the deck of the ship with her baby in her arms, she leaned against the rails to look at the fish in the water, her infant slipped out of her hands and fell into the ocean. She started crying for help, an Indian gentleman, risked his own life and jumped into the ocean and saved her baby. When the news had reached the captain of the ship, he said, "That is love. They had never met each other but when she cried for help, he jumped into the ocean to save her child. That is true sacrifice. Hence, this evening, in honor of our Indian hero we will have a special dinner sponsored by the captain." At dinner there was plenty of food, music, and dance. Once again the captain thanked him profusely. Finally, the captain turned to the Indian gentleman and asked him, "Is there anything that you would like to say?" The Indian picked up the microphone and said, "I have been waiting the entire day for this moment. I demand to know who pushed me into the ocean?"

The French lady was so grateful that he had saved her child; it did not matter to her who pushed him into the water.

It has been said that gratitude is a feeling of the heart. If the heart is the seat of God's wisdom, a place where love originates, then it is fitting and proper that gratitude should also arise from the heart and not from the mind. Blaise Pascal said, "The heart has reason that reason does not know." The mind can justify, rationalize, analyze, demand, and take for granted the kind gestures that others do for us, but it is only the heart for reasons known and unknown that is capable of bursting forth in love and gratitude.

Jesus and the Ten Lepers

The gospel of Luke narrates an interesting event in the life of Jesus that highlights the meaning of gratitude:

> And as he entered a village, he was met by ten lepers, who stood at a distance and lifted up their voices and said, "Jesus, Master, have mercy on us." When he saw them he said to them, "Go and show yourselves to the priests." And as they went they were cleansed. Then one of them, when he saw that he was healed, turned back, praising God with a loud voice; and he fell on his face

at Jesus' feet, giving him thanks. Now he was a Samaritan. Then said Jesus, "Were not ten cleansed? Where are the nine? Was no one found to return and give praise to God except this foreigner?" And he said to him, "Rise and go your way; your faith has made you well" (Lk 17: 12-19).

It is reasonable then to ask, did the other nine do anything wrong by not returning to Jesus to thank him? It was Jesus who asked them to go and show themselves to the priests at the temple. They obeyed the words of Jesus; nevertheless, he goes on to say, "Were not ten cleansed? Where are the nine? Was no one found to return and give praise to God except this foreigner" (Lk 17:17-18)? During the time of Jesus, people with contagious diseases lived outside the society and by law they had to maintain physical distance from other people. Hence, when someone was cured, the law demanded that they had to be declared clean and pure by the priests and offer the necessary offerings at the temple in order to be reinstated into the society. It is against this background that Jesus tells them to go and show themselves to the priests. On their way not only the Samaritan experienced a healing, but also the other nine lepers experienced a miracle. While the other nine went ahead to fulfill the law, only the Samaritan returned to give thanks to Jesus. Jesus praises him. Why?

The act of the Samaritan highlights the importance of being grateful and expressing one's gratitude over fulfillment of religious obligations, rituals, and rules. It is not that Jesus is playing down the importance of fulfilling religious obligations. One could fulfill religious obligations for the sake of fulfilling them but still not think of God and be grateful to God for healing them. Probably, for a long time, these people had been suffering from leprosy. They were not only "unapproachables," but also socially, religiously, and culturally they were considered outcasts as well. No one wanted to associate with them. They were shunned both by their families and the society. It was indeed a miserable life. In their cry, Jesus not only sees their leprosy, but also their rejection by society. Jesus felt compassion for them, and it is from his compassionate heart that he reaches out to them and heals them.

Jesus told them to go and show themselves to the priests in the temple. When healing takes place, the Samaritan realized that gratitude to the one who healed him was far more important than the fulfillment of the ritual that was expected of him. Probably he must have thought to himself, "There is plenty of time to go to the temple and show myself to the priests, but I must return immediately and express my gratitude to the one who has healed me." We may not understand the full significance of the healing that the Samaritan experienced because it was not only physical healing, but also more than that, it was being accepted back into society, to be considered and treated as a human being. It was life, a second life given back to him. If not for Jesus, he would have still continued to live a miserable life as a leper. He owed his life and everything to Jesus. That is why gratitude for him was far more important than the immediate fulfillment of the rituals. No wonder he returned to give thanks to Jesus.

Human memory is so short that we tend to forget the good that others have done to us. The worst part of the human memory is that it remembers the hurts, the resentments, and the negativities that others have caused us and what others have failed to do for us. Why is it so difficult to be grateful? Why do we take for granted the good and kindness that others have done for us? What are the ways by which we can express our gratitude? How can we grow to be grateful?

Why should we be grateful?

A fundamental truth of life is that life is a balance between uniqueness and dependence. We are each unique beings. God has created us unique. God loves variety. Isn't it amazing that in the entire history of humanity, God has not created another human being just like you. When God decides to create a human life, God does not walk down a hall looking at human replicas to reproduce a human being. In all eternity we are unique human beings, and life is a celebration of one's uniqueness. While we are all unique, we also realize that we are also social beings. We are born into this world with the union of two people in love. Even for our birth we depended on our parents to be co-creators with God. Don't we depend on others, at birth, to help us in the passage of birth, and at death to carry our casket? From the womb to the tomb life is a constant dependency on others.

We depend on others because as individuals it is impossible to do everything by ourselves. We continually depend upon the services of others. An ordinary day in our life begins with the help of others. We depend on:

> - the labor of PG&E workers who continue to supply us with electricity and gas.
> - the newspaper carrier to provide us with the newspaper.
> - the coffee that warms our bodies is the result of many people's work.
> - the bread and the cereals that strengthen our bodies are products of not just one person.
> - the water that serves our various purposes, the clean clothes that we wear, the car or the public transportation that takes us from one place to another, the materials and the tools that we use at work are all the result of the labor of many human beings.
> - the many things throughout the day we use that are made possible to us by others.
> - the doctors and health care professionals we depend on, farmers, plumbers, electricians, postal carriers, priests whose services we need; spouses depend on each other, children depend on their parents, the elderly on the state, the police, the fire department personnel, the security, and so on.

In life we constantly depend on others. It is true that we are individuals, yet at the same time we are social beings who depend on the services of many others. Dependence is a healthy balance between individualism and collectivism. We need both; for life is possible only in the balance between the two. The more we realize this, the more we will understand how much our life is dependent on others. It is indeed difficult to manage life on our own. We need others, their help and services. Our life is beautiful because there are many people who do so much for us that we normally take for granted. We can focus on our goals and dreams only because we enjoy the fruits of the works of others. For me this is the first reason why we should be grateful because alone, by ourselves, we cannot achieve much in life. We depend on others. We need others.

Our own limitations are manifested by our dependence on others. Gratitude is nothing more than acknowledging our own limitations and our dependence on others. In a way it is saying, *"I need you. My life is beautiful because of you."* Gratitude is an acceptance of our own insufficiency and an affirmation of our dependence on others.

"Interbeing" according to Thich Nhat Hanh expresses this reality. We are all connected to each other and every thing in nature is connected with the other. Following his line of thinking, for example, when I drink a cup of coffee, I must realize that it is not just the coffee that I am drinking, but along with the coffee, the labor of the people that have picked the beans,

those who have dried them, ground them, watered the plants, the sunshine, the fertilizers, the shade of the trees, and many other factors that have gone into making this cup of coffee that I am drinking. Gratitude is the realization of this interbeing, interconnectedness, and interdependence. When we drink a cup of coffee, we take for granted the sacrifice and work that has gone into the making of the cup of coffee. Also, does not a cup of coffee reveal the entire universe to me? Coffee as such does not exist alone. Similarly, we are all connected to each other. It is not possible to live without this connectedness and relatedness. Gratitude is the recognition and affirmation of this interconnectedness and interbeing.

If we depend on others and we need their help, then how much more we need to acknowledge our constant dependence on God. When we realize this dependence on God, we cannot help being grateful to God. Our very life is a gift from God. We did not create ourselves. God created us and brought us into this life. When we are grateful to God, it is this that we acknowledge. We acknowledge our constant dependence on God. We are nothing without God. Are we not constantly held in the palm of God's hands? Nothing happens in our life without God's knowledge. Whenever we think of God, only thanks and gratitude should arise within our hearts.

Why are we not grateful?

In the first place, if gratitude has not become a virtue in us, it is probably because most often *we take for granted* the benefits that we constantly receive from others. We may feel and justify to ourselves that it is the duty of the other person to do certain things for us. For e.g., a husband may take his wife for granted by expecting her to do for him without even being asked or by not appreciating what she may do for him and vice versa. Children may feel that it is their right and it is the duty of the parents to look after them and to provide for them, or the parents may think that it is their right and it is the duty of the children to look after them in their old age. Gratitude is not possible as long as the concepts of right and duty qualify our relationships and our service for each other. We keep demanding that others should serve us, and we tend to take for granted their service for us. It is my right to expect it, and it is their duty to do it. Even if it is the obligation of the other person, as long as we depend on others and we still benefit from their time, labor, and service, then we really should be grateful.

Secondly, if we are not grateful, it is because we are not genuinely contented with what we have. A contented heart is a grateful heart, but human nature seems to want more and more. Often we are not satisfied with what we have. At times, in our life, don't we suffer from the "wanting more syndrome?" What we possess does not seem to satisfy our human hearts. It is the desire for more and more that prevents us from being grateful. Falsely, we think that the more we have, the happier we will be, but the desire for more is an unquenchable craving. In the Indian religious literature *Shiva Purana,* Shiva is a wandering mendicant who uses a *Kapala* (a begging bowl). Whatever is put inside the bowl, the bowl then immediately swallows, leaving the bowl empty. Like the *Kapala,* there is never an end to our desires. Little do we realize that the more we want, the more we are going to feel sad and suffer as a result. We are seldom able to be satisfied with what we have. *Rather than looking at what we have and being contented and grateful, we seem to often focus on what we don't have and that causes us to suffer.*

A person who totally relies on God's divine providence will always be grateful to God for what that person receives. We do not deserve it. Imagine if we are on the street and someone takes pity on us and helps us to have a comfortable life in the society, would we not always remain grateful to the person who has helped us? This is also true in our relationship with God. From nothingness God created us and has given us this life and all that we have. For a person of faith, everything is a gratuitous gift from God. Because it is a gift from God, we will always be contented with what God gives us and remain grateful to God. When we are contented and grateful, God will continue to take care of us. This is what the author of the letter to the Hebrews said, "Keep your life free from love of money, and be content with what you have; ..." (Heb 13:5). Gratitude is the acknowledgement of our dependence on God. God can never sufficiently be thanked. It is not that God is going to increase in Godliness because of our gratitude or decrease in Godliness when we are ungrateful. Irrespective of our gratitude or lack thereof,

God remains God. When we do thank God, we express our dependence and continuously learn to surrender our life in trust to God.

When gratitude becomes our life, we will stop grumbling and complaining. We will be able to accept with serenity even the hardships that occur in life. A person without gratitude is like the son who complained to his father about his shoes, until he saw a man without legs. When we make a habit of being grateful, even when life seems to be tough and hard, then even what is rough and difficult will reveal truths of life and existence to us. There was a famous Sufi mystic who at the end of each day would always thank nature for what he had received from it. Once it happened that he and his disciples had to go without food and water for a few days. They were not welcomed in any village; they were despised, hated, and even stoned. Every evening as usual the mystic would thank nature for blessing him with wonderful gifts. This was too much for the disciples to accept, and hence they confronted him, "Master, how can you be thankful to nature when all that we have received from nature is rejection, thirst, hunger, hatred, stones, etc?" The master replied, "Yes, we received nothing but stones, hunger, thirst, and hatred. Villages rejected us. When all these things were happening I realized that there was no anger or revenge or hatred within me. I felt no animosity towards them. On the contrary, I feel sorry for their ignorance and I only have compassion for them. I am grateful to nature because it has revealed this to me. Nature always contains truths and is willing to reveal them to us. If we are grateful to what nature gives us, it will also reveal truths to us." The Sufi master was right. When we are grateful, we will always celebrate life no matter what life may bring.

Often we are accustomed to perceive the negative that is wrong in a situation than what is positive, beautiful and right in the situation. If only we have eyes to see, we will see beauty and rays of hope everywhere even in situations that appear to be bleak and hopeless. Two prisoners who were in the same prison cell looked through the same window. While one saw only dust and dirt and cursed God, the other looked through the same window and saw the bright twinkling stars in the blue sky and thanked God. It is a question of our perception with which we look at the reality. We can see only the bad and gripe about it, or even in the apparent bad we can perceive good, and be grateful to God. Reality is never one-dimensional. It does not permit only one perception or interpretation. It depends on how we look, and what we are looking for.

How should we be grateful?

> We should always remember to thank people from whom we have benefited. One of the best ways to remember those who have done favors for us is to remember them in our prayers. Let us never forget to acknowledge and appreciate what others have done for us. Do not forget to send a note of thanks or flowers to acknowledge the good deeds that others have done for us. It is not so much what we have

received, but the attitude with which we have received and the remembrance to say a simple "thanks." Let us try to cultivate the habit of saying thanks always. Never take for granted and assume it is the duty of the other person to do a favor for us.

➢ Just as we have received benefits from others, whenever opportunities arise, we should do what we can do to help others. In our daily lives there are so many occasions in which we can benefit the lives of others. Just as we have reaped the benefits from the gracious actions of others, may others benefit from our selfless deeds. Let gratitude be like a river. Like the river, let it flow. Let it constantly flow and keep flowing. Let it never stop.

➢ Another way of being grateful is to share what God has given us. If God has blessed us with many things, we need to share those with others. In sharing what we have and what we are, gratitude continues. Let us not only be receivers, but let us also learn to share and to give to others. There is great joy in giving, and it is better to give than to receive. It is said that once God sent two angels to the earth with two baskets. One basket was marked, *"Petitions"* and the other was marked *"Thank You."* The angels went throughout the earth. When the angels returned to heaven, the *"petition basket"* was over flowing with requests, but the *"thank you basket"* was empty. Not even one note of thanks.

➢ It would be a good idea to have a *"gratitude day"* in our life. While all days should be days of gratitude, still we could choose a day as a *"gratitude day"* to live constantly in the awareness of being truly grateful for each and everything that we have been blessed with.

➢ Let us learn to look at everything in the universe as if it were created just for us. The blue sky, the white fluffy clouds, the twinkling stars, the gentle breeze, the sprinkling of the rain, the blooming of flowers, the different seasons, the song of the birds, the dance of the leaves, the rising waves, the sunrise and the sunset. All of these were meant just for us. When we are filled with the thought that God has created all these only for us, won't our hearts be filled with gratitude? If we are in the habit of thanking God for everything that happens in our life, then there is really no room for misery, but only moments of celebration and joy.

➢ Throughout the day let gratitude constantly be in our hearts and on our lips. During meals, in the silence of our hearts, always thank all those who have made it possible for the food that is on our plate. As we drive our cars, remember to thank all of those who have assembled the various parts. May the clothes we are wearing bring a sense of gratitude for those who weaved and manufactured them. And so on...

> Today we should either call or write to all of those who have helped us, and thank them. We should do this before it is too late.
> Pray the wonderful Psalms of thanksgiving. Try making the prayer of the psalmist our very own. In all situations as St. Paul said, let us with a grateful heart learn to rejoice, "Rejoice in the Lord always; again I will say, Rejoice. Let all men know your forbearance. The Lord is at hand. Have no anxiety about anything, but in everything by prayer and supplication with thanksgiving let your requests be made known to God" (Phil 4:4-6).
> Let us not forget to thank our creator. Try to begin your day with gratitude and end each day with gratitude, as well as throughout the day, let our hearts be raised in gratitude to God.

Thank God:

> For the gift of life
> For the gift of faith
> For creation with all its beauty and wonder
> For the beauty of the human body
> For the mind that is so fascinating
> For the gift of human sexuality
> For the wonder of human conception
> For health
> For our families
> For our spouses and children
> For friends and family

> ➤ For science and technology
> ➤ For the inventions of the human mind
> ➤ For God's presence in our life
> ➤ For all our experiences, joyful and sad

An atheist was walking through a forest and he heard a noise behind him. As he turned to see what the noise was, to his great surprise, he saw a lion following him. He walked faster and the lion walked faster also. He ran and the lion ran after him, as he ran faster, the lion ran faster and knocked him down. As the lion was standing above him, he cried, "Oh God." He heard a voice from the sky say, "I thought you always said that I did not exist." The man replied, "Hey God, I am not praying to turn me into a believer. I am praying that you turn the lion into a Christian." "So be it," said God. Immediately the lion folded its hands and said, "Oh God, bless this food which I am about to receive and for which I am truly thankful. Amen."

In all circumstances learn to be grateful to God

O God!

You have formed me in my mother's womb and consecrated me to yourself even before I had known you.

You have called me by name and placed me in the palm of your hands.

You have created me out of nothingness.

You have given me this beautiful life and the gift of faith.

You have always watched over me and kept me safe.

Oh God, when I think of you, how can I remain ungrateful?

My heart bursts with gratitude to you, O God.

Let me always acknowledge my dependence on you alone.

Let me learn to trust in your divine providence.

Bless me with a contented heart that is always full of gratitude.

May I learn to rejoice with what I have.

Let me never take for granted the benefits that I receive from others.

Just as I have received, may I now learn to share.

Let gratitude flow through me.

May I become gratitude.

Sharing: Being Godlike

> *for I was hungry and you gave me food,*
> *I was thirsty and you gave me drink,*
> *I was a stranger and you welcomed me,*
> *I was naked and you clothed me,*
> *I was sick and you visited me,*
> *I was in prison and you came to me.*
>
> ...
>
> *Truly, I say to you, as you did it*
> *to one of the least of these my brethren,*
> *you did it to me.*
>
> —Mt: 25:35-36,40

The Bible and Love for Riches

In the gospel of Luke, Jesus narrates the parable of Lazarus and the rich man:

> There was a rich man, who was clothed in purple and fine linen and feasted sumptuously each day. And at his gate lay a poor man named Lazarus, full of sores, who desired to be fed with what fell from the rich man's table; moreover the dogs came and licked his sores. The poor man died and was carried by the angels to Abraham's bosom. The rich man also died and was buried; and in Hades, being in torment, ... (Lk 16:19-23).

When I read this story, over and over again my attention returned to Jesus when he said that when Lazarus died he went to heaven, and when the rich man died he went to the fires of hell. Why was Jesus so strong in condemning the rich man to hell? What did the rich man do to deserve punishment in hell? Is God partial to the poor? Will only the poor reach heaven? Not just in this parable does Jesus seem to be very strong against the rich and their riches, but elsewhere in the gospels also, he appears to feel very strongly against the rich and their riches:

> ➤ "But woe to you that are rich..." (Lk 6:24).
> ➤ "Again I tell you, it is easier for a camel to go through the eye of a needle than for a rich man to enter the kingdom of God" (Mt 19:24).
> ➤ In the parable of the rich man building large barns to store all his grains and goods, Jesus says, "... 'Fool! This night your soul is required of you; and the things you have prepared, whose will they be?' " (Lk 12:20).
> ➤ "The rich man also died and was buried; and in Hades, being in torment, ..." (Lk 16:22-23).
> ➤ "Do not lay up for yourselves treasures on earth..." (Mt 6:19).
> ➤ "... but the cares of the world and the delight in riches choke the word, and it proves unfruitful" (Mt 13:22).
> ➤ "... You cannot serve God and mammon" (Mt 6:24).

These sayings of Jesus may give us the impression that Jesus was against the rich and their riches. This would completely misinterpret the meaning of Jesus' radical teaching on being open to the Reign of God.

Though Jesus made an option for the poor, it was not an option that excluded others. Jesus reached out to all who welcomed him and listened to his call to experience inner conversion. Thus, there is the conversion of those who held financial power (Matthew and Zachaeus), and those who enjoyed political and religious powers (Joseph of Arimathea and Nicodemus). Jesus admired the faith of the centurion and was ready to go to his house. Jesus accepted the services of the women who served him. He even allowed himself to be anointed with the most expensive ointment.

The Bible does not teach that money is the root of evil but, that *"... love of money is the root of all evils"* (1Tim 6:10). There is a vast difference between the two. Money in itself is not evil. It can be used either for good or bad purposes. It all depends on how we use it. In today's world we cannot fulfill the fundamental needs of our family without money. We work and we are remunerated for our work. We live and help those who are dependent on us to live with the remuneration we receive for our hard and honest work. It is the *love* of money that is the root of all evil. The question that remains is, in what sense is love of money the root of all evils?

The Bible teaches us that one cannot serve both God and money; both must not be the first passion in our lives. Primacy of one in our life is relegating the other to a lower level. It is a question of choice. There is every possibility that money can become our first passion and love in our life. If love of money is the top priority on our list of values, then it becomes evil. Jesus says, "For where your treasure is, there will your heart be also" (Lk 12:34). If God is our treasure beyond all other treasures, then it is with God that our hearts will be. God becomes the alpha and the omega of our life. When God becomes the focus of our life, then money assumes its proper value as well. St. Paul writing to Timothy warns us:

> But those who desire to be rich fall into the temptation, into a snare, into many senseless and hurtful desires that plunge men into ruin and destruction. For the love of money is the root of all evils; it is through this craving that some have wandered away from the faith and pierced their hearts with many pangs (1Tim 6:9-10).

When the love of money becomes the center of our life, as St. Paul said, then we become victims of temptation and harmful desire, we expose ourselves to ruin, destruction, and various pains, and it will take us away from our faith and God. Money is evil when it becomes a great obstacle in surrendering ourselves to God. When our hearts are set on money and all that it can bring, then we will never be free to experience the fruit of personal, spiritual, and moral conversion. Because of the diametrically opposed nature of the values of the Reign of God and love for riches, the human person will not be able to experience the reality of the Reign of God, which Jesus offers to each one of us. In the story of the young rich man, when Jesus told him to go and sell everything and give it all to the poor, then come and follow him, the young man went away sad because he had many possessions and his attachment to his possessions was the hindrance.

Riches, if not seen in their proper perspective and not properly handled, will not only take us away from God, but it can also create a false sense of security, complacency, pride, and vain glory. When Jesus says, "Blessed are the poor in spirit, for theirs is the kingdom of heaven" (Mt 5:3) Jesus is not glorifying or spiritualizing physical poverty and misery. Rather because of their poverty, the poor are totally dependent on God alone. God is their only source of strength, security, and sole provider. Their lives revolve around God's divine providence and goodness. Rather than turning to God and glorifying God, riches have the effect of turning us inward to look into ourselves and glorify our own talents and strengths. Riches can sometimes result in a lack of openness, awareness, and dependence upon God.

Jesus experienced tremendous inner freedom because his lifestyle was simple. For Jesus, God was his only security. "Look at the birds of the air: they neither sow nor reap nor gather into barns, and yet your heavenly Father feeds them..." (Mt 6:26). For a person whose possessions are plenty, his attachments are also great. And where there is attachment there can never be true freedom. Not only is there lack of inner freedom, but also there is avariciousness, dishonesty, greed, and injustice. At times, when one's heart is set on riches alone, the means used to obtain riches can become evil. Thus, it is not a question of the end justifying the means.

Riches will also create a false sense of security and power. Here again Jesus stands as a great model. He did not have any security or power. His only power and security was God. In the desert when the devil tempted him and offered him power, Jesus refused, but chose to rely on God alone. Throughout his public life when people wanted him to assume social and political power, Jesus refused to give in to their wishes. From the cross, he was asked to use his power to come down, but he placed his total unconditional trust in God alone and God vindicated his trust. Jesus emptied himself of everything, the desire to possess, to dominate, and to control others. St. Paul writing to the Philippians says:

> Have this mind among yourselves, which was in Christ Jesus, who, though he was in the form of God, did not count equality with God a thing to be grasped, but emptied himself, taking the form of a servant, being born in the likeness of men. And being found in human form he humbled himself and became obedient unto death, even death on a cross (Phil 2:5-7).

His emptiness not only freed him from attachments to material things, but also gave him true inner freedom, a freedom that enabled him to open himself totally to God's gratuitous love and also to others.

Love of riches can take us away not only from God, but also from our family and relationships. When money preoccupies our hearts and minds, then we don't have time for others, starting with our own family. Before going to bed a little boy asked his father, "Daddy, tell me how much money you make in one hour?" "I make $100 an hour," said his Daddy proudly. "Daddy, I will give you $100 that I have managed to save for the past year. Then could you please spend one hour with me?" How sad, but true. Often times parents are so busy trying to earn money for necessities and extra things they tend to lose sight of what is really important and neglect spending time with their children. How many families are destroyed, relationships broken, marriages on the rocks, and children grow up with violence and anger, rarely seeing their parents except on the weekends? Riches can buy most of the things in the world, but not family, love, relationships, or human values such as compassion, mercy, sharing, caring, respect for human dignity, and honesty.

One of the reasons for the rich man's failure was that his heart was set on riches and not on God. Why do we make such a strong claim? Because, a person who is really open to God, will surely share his riches with others, especially with the people that are less fortunate. One who serves money has no place for God, but for one who serves God, money falls in its proper place, that is, the need to share with others. Jesus says, "... You received without pay, give without pay" (Mt 10:8). The riches blinded the rich man from seeing God in Lazarus. Lazarus did not exist in his life at all. He was completely indifferent to the presence of poor

Lazarus sitting by his gate. He must have passed through those gates so many times, yet Lazarus was a nonentity to him. The cry of Lazarus did not fall on his ears.

Indifference and ignoring poor Lazarus is another cause for the rich man's failure. Little do we realize that God will not remain indifferent to the cry of the poor. God did not remain a silent witness to the oppression, exploitation, and slavery of his people in Egypt. At their cry, God sent Moses to tell Pharaoh, "... I have seen the oppression with which the Egyptians oppress them. Come, I will send you to Pharaoh that you may bring forth my people" (Ex 3:9-10). God not only frees them from physical slavery, but also accompanies them on their journey as "cloud by day and fire by night" (Ex 13:21-22) and leads them to the Promised Land. In the Promised Land, when people began to oppress and exploit the poor, God chose the prophets to defend the rights of the poor and also to bring condemnation against the oppressors. God was their only defender. God makes a preferential option of the *anawim* (the widows, the poor, the orphans, and the aliens). God is on the side of the victims of injustice and oppression (Lev 19:33; Ex 22:21; Is 3:14-15; Amos 2:6; 8:4-8; 4:1). The prophet's criticisms were severe against the priests who interpreted the laws to their own advantage to exploit the poor (Is 10:1-2; Jer 22: 3). God did not spare the judges who favored the rich in their judgments (Amos 5:12). The establishment of the monarchy and the merchant class that exploited the poor and their labor did not escape the wrath of God (1 Sam 8:12-5). The prophets spoke vehemently against the entire religious-social-political-cultural system that took advantage of the poor. God was the only defender of the poor.

Jesus, in the New Testament continues the mission of the Old Testament prophets. Jesus, like God in the Old Testament, does make an option for the poor. Such an option is manifested both in his personal and public life. Jesus grew up in a despised village. In his public ministry he lived poorly with no place to lay his head down; he depended on others. He related to ordinary folks, and scandalized the hierarchy by his table fellowship with the social outcasts, and finally through misuse of power, he was put to death unjustly.

Jesus was very severe in his criticism of the Pharisees and the scribes who interpreted the laws of Moses to their own advantage and that of the rich. Jesus challenged the misuse of their power and authority. He constantly questioned the authorities that manipulated religious, political, and financial power for their own advantage. He continually criticized both the religious and social aristocracies of his time that combined together to take advantage of the poor and the marginalized.

A disciple of Jesus is not called to exercise power, but to be servants willing to serve others. They are those who are willing to share their wealth and resources with others, especially the poor. This is how others saw the early Christian community (Acts 4:32-35). Jesus' true disciples are those who are willing to be self-emptied and are prepared to let go the social, religious, political, monetary powers; the desire to possess, to dominate, to control; and to take places of prestige in the market places and in the synagogues. They are those who are gentle and humble. It is possible, because their hearts are set on God alone and that is exactly why they could serve and share their goods with others, especially the poor.

God of Incarnation: Its Implications

In God's option for the poor and reaching out to them, *God does not act alone.* God acts through other human beings. In the Old Testament God acted through Moses and the prophets and in the New Testament through His son Jesus Christ, whose incarnation continues through all those who continue his mission. Ron Rolheiser, in his *Holy Longing,* points out that the incarnation of God continues even to this day through the Body of Christ, which includes Jesus, the body of believers, and in the celebration of the Eucharist. Thus, according to him, not only God in heaven is being petitioned to answer our prayers, but we too, as the body of Christ assume responsibility to answer the prayers of our brothers and sisters, especially the cry of the poor. This is to give "incarnational flesh, skin to our prayer." Someone had beautifully said it, "God, who created the world without us, cannot continue to save the world without us." God who hears the cry of the poor cannot reach out to the poor without the help of fellow human beings.

St. Teresa of Avila, in a very simple language, captures what we are trying to say:

Christ has no body but yours,
No hands but yours,
No feet but yours.
Yours are the eyes through which
Christ's compassion must look out on the world.
Yours are the feet with which
He is to go about doing good.
Yours are the hands with which
He is to bless now.

Like the prophet Habukkuk, the poor cry out to God, "O LORD, how long shall I cry for help, and thou wilt not hear? Or cry to thee 'Violence!' and thou wilt not save? Why dost thou make me see wrongs and look upon trouble? Destruction and violence are before me; strife and contention arise" (Hab 1:2-3). God's help can reach the poor only through other human beings. God cannot intervene unless we are prepared to intervene. It is only through us that God is able to intervene. Through Jesus' incarnation God reached out to us. The continuation of God's incarnation solely depends upon us.

It follows that when the poor cry to God, God expects us to act. If we take the story of incarnation seriously then we have no other alternative than to act on behalf of the poor and the underprivileged. This is where the rich man failed. He failed to see in Lazarus the very God he was worshipping in the synagogue. He failed to be an extension of God, failing to give God flesh to be incarnated again. A person who is selfish cannot behold God in others, especially the poor. Where there is selfishness, there cannot be any ground for compassion or willingness to share, for compassion and willingness to share are truly qualities of God.

Bishop Thomas Gumbleton, after returning from a visit to Haiti, shared his reflection in his homily:

> I'll tell you, when I was in Haiti and I was in that jail, something happened that overwhelmed me. I was looking into the cell and finding it very difficult. I just could not imagine what it meant to be in that cell 24 hours a day, and suddenly it was as though I saw Jesus right there in the cell. I had to turn away and walk away because I was overwhelmed with the thought. First of all, I thought of how wrong this is! Yet, on the other hand, it was clear that Jesus totally identifies with us. He was in that cell. He is in that cell. Jesus enters into every bit of oppression and suffering that we have ever experienced, because we are members of God's household.

The God we worship is not only in the temples, churches, and mosques, but God is everywhere, especially in the poor and the outcasts of the society. In the Acts of the Apostles, when Saul was on his way to Damascus to persecute the Christians, he fell by a great light from heaven and he heard a voice say, "Saul, Saul, why do you persecute me?" and he said, "Who are you, Lord?" And he said, "I am Jesus, whom you are persecuting; ..." (Acts 9:4-5). God identifies himself in a very special way with the poor, because God is their only defender. The greatest challenge is to see the face of God in the poor and the suffering. St. Martin of Tours, while returning to the city, found at the city gate an old man who was shivering in the cold. Martin took pity on him and cut his cloak into two and gave one-half to the old man. That night in a dream, Martin saw Jesus wearing one-half of the cloak he had given to the poor man. Mother Teresa once said, "Would you not serve the poor like they were Jesus? We should serve the poor *because they **are** Jesus*." It calls for a tremendous act of faith not just to see the presence of God, but also to see God himself in the poor.

Probably, the rich man in the story was a good man too. He must have been involved in the committees of the synagogues, in the various welfare programs for his community, a regular worshipper of God, keeping the commandments of God... yet in the eyes of Jesus he failed because he was unable to see God in Lazarus whom he passed by everyday. At least, the dog had pity on him by licking his sores and bringing comfort to him. The dog did what it could. The rich man could have done much more, but he chose to be indifferent. He was not moved with compassion. Without genuine compassion sharing is not possible.

Compassion is not a feeling of pity or feeling of empathy. It is a stirring within the heart, a movement that results in an action. When Jesus saw the crowd following him for days, Jesus was moved with compassion and said to his disciples, "They need not go away; you give them something to eat" (Mt 14:16). When he saw the widow of Naim, his heart was filled with compassion. Out of this compassion for her he acted (Lk 7:13). Compassion is not just a feeling of pity for the poor and the marginalized, but a decision to do something to help and to make a difference for those in need. The rich man had resources, but he did not care enough to share his riches. He could have done something, but he chose to be selfish and not do anything.

It was curfew time in Kolkatta, India. Mother Teresa was informed that one of the families in the same area had lost their father in the shootout. She took a bag of rice with her to meet the family. She gave the bag of rice to the mother and asked her to cook some rice for her children. The woman took the bag and disappeared and did not return for sometime. When she finally returned Mother Teresa said to her, "I thought you would cook some rice and give it to your children, but you seem to have disappeared." She said, "Mother, there is another family a few houses away that also lost their father; the children in that family have not eaten for several days. When you gave me the bag of rice, I realized that just as you shared this bag of rice with me, I too need to share with the other family as well." It is easy to give from one's abundance, but to give when it hurts is really much more difficult. The real meaning of sharing lies precisely in this.

Some might think, "There is tremendous global poverty. What can I do as an individual to change the situation?" Indeed a very logical and realistic question. A while back I happened to see the movie, *When Did I See You Hungry?* a very inspiring and moving video presentation on global poverty. The following statistics are taken from the video presentation:

> Every minute of every day 20 children die of hunger or diseases related to hunger
> Two-thirds of humanity lives in crippling poverty
> Globally about 800 million people do not have access to adequate food and nutrition. Of those, 200 million are children.
> 300 million people subsist on less than 65 cents a day
> In America 700,000 people are without shelter on any given night
> In Africa 15% of children die before age 5
> 20% of the world's population consumes 85% of all goods and services; the poorest 20% consumes 1%
> 20,000 to 40,000 children under the age 5 will die from the economic consequences of September 11, 2001.

These figures can overwhelm and frighten us. We can choose to back away and say, "It is too much for an individual or an organization to do something to make an impact." Let the governments, various organizations do whatever they have to do, but the question is: What is my personal response? In what way can God continue to reach out to the poorest of the poor? What is something that I can do? The real problem is that we hope and pray that others will come forward and do something instead of us. We depend on others to always share, but when it comes to us to share our gifts, talents, resources, and time we avoid it and shun away. A pastor was asking the people in his congregation for donations to build a new church. At collection time one man thought to himself. "Well, everyone will be writing a check to cover the expenses of a new church, therefore if I put a blank piece of paper into the collection basket, no one will ever notice." When they were counting the money from the collection that had been taken, much to the pastors' surprise everyone else had thought and responded in the same manner. Do not wait for others to act; instead we should take the initiative.

In *The Daily Review* of Thursday, May 16, 2002 there was an article about Shayna Parekh, a top graduating student from the University of California, Berkeley. She was awarded the highest academic award – the University Medal. The article portrayed her as "a charming, verbal, brilliant young woman." Shayna is a native of Southern California. Born in Long Beach, her parents had migrated to the U.S. from India. What caught my attention when I was reading this article was that while she was continuing her studies, during the summer, she found time to work with the abandoned babies at Mother Teresa's Children's Home. The previous summer she had returned to India to work as a volunteer helping with the earthquake relief in Bhuj, Gujarat, India. She managed to set up a literacy program, working with the worker's children, teaching them to read and write. This program gradually expanded to include adults also. After graduating she planned to return to India to do voluntary work for one year at *Veerayatan,* a non-profit organization and then continue her studies. As I read about her involvement with the poor, it also called to my mind the many college students from other countries that have come to India during their summer holidays to work for the street children. Their interest and commitment was really outstanding and praise worthy. They came to be with, and to give their time to the poor and in the process; they too, were enriched by the poor. A couple who are retired wanting to do something for the poor find time every year to return to the Philippines to care for the street children. Instead of enjoying their well-deserved retirement, they put their resources, time, energy, and presence at the service of these children. Although their own family would like them to be living comfortably in the U.S., they feel that being with and helping these street children is what God is calling them to do at this time in their lives.

Both Shayna, and the youth who worked with the poor could have taken the summer off to relax from the demands of the academic world; they could have gone to wonderful locations. The retired couple could live their retirement catching up with old friends, being surrounded by family and friends, and living a comfortable life-style in the U.S., but they realized that they have to give back to others what they have received, especially the poor and the abandoned. I have witnessed and continue to observe many wonderful human beings who often reach out and help the poor. Their help comes not from their abundance, but from their own sacrifices and constant "denials."

"It is better to light a candle than to curse the darkness." It is easy to blame the oppressive situations on the policies of the government, and the bureaucracy. It is true that alone we cannot change the world, but there is something that each one of us can and should do in order to make a difference. Even if it may seem insignificant, you can have a positive effect on the lives of those who are less fortunate. As Mother Teresa said, *"Do small things with great love."*

Some Things That All of Us Can Do

Pray for the gift of God's grace and light for each of us to become sensitive and aware of the needs, situation, and condition of the poor. The greatest tragedy that we can bring upon ourselves is our own indifference to the situation of the poor. In the light of faith or convictions, reflect on a possible response to the situation. Wherever we are, we can find circumstances where we can offer our assistance to others. Look right in the place where we live and we can find so many opportunities to give of ourselves to help others and respond to their needs.

Learn to share your talents, gifts, resources, wealth, possessions, love, and time. There are enough resources on this earth for everyone. It is said that the amount of money that is invested in the production of arms on this earth is sufficient to feed every single mouth three times a day for one full year. We have enough natural resources, but what we lack is the true spirit of sharing. Share until it hurts. It is easy to share from our abundance, but it is difficult for us to be generous with our own possessions, when we are uncertain of what we may have tomorrow. Let us give without expecting anything in return. When we give and share we should not wish, even in the remotest part of our unconscious mind, that God should bless us or even return our sharing hundred-fold. While it is true that God will bless us, and the good that we do for others will return to us, the motivation with which we share should not be for the intention of being rewarded a hundred-fold in return. Let there be purity in sharing. There is truly more joy in giving than in receiving. The joy that we experience when we share without expecting anything in return is a pure joy. For when we share, the angels in heaven are smiling because we become like God.

Do not be a spectator. Be involved. There are many activities that we could become involved in. It could be volunteering in a hospital, a visit to the convalescent hospitals, to talk with people whom no one visits, to push the wheel chair for someone who awaits the whole day to be moved around, to bring flowers to the lonely, to place a telephone call to someone who is lonely, to help the elderly with chores that are difficult, to teach someone to read, to accompany children to visit their mothers in prison, to visit a sick person, to be kind and sensitive to the elderly, the disabled, and the homeless, to join a St. Vincent de Paul organization, to work in a soup kitchen, to organize a clothing/toy drive, to join *"make a difference"* program, to take up the cause of refugees, to join a fund raiser, write to state representatives in support of programs for the poor... There are situations right in the areas where we live.

Live a simple life. The Bible does not teach us to embrace poverty or embrace a life of misery. The earth and all the things of the earth are given to us for our well-being. While we are not called to a life of misery, we are definitely called to lead a simple life. There is far more to life then material things. We do not want to become slaves to our own possessions. Let our life be determined by our needs and not our wants. As human beings all of us have our fundamental needs to be met and we have a right to our basic needs. A list of wants can keep increasing as our desires keep increasing. A list of wants is based on craving more and more and on dissatisfaction and discontentment with what we already have. The list of wants never decreases. As technology keeps developing and the market is filled with more and more sophisticated goods, our list of wants will only keep increasing. For example I can use a car for a number of years or I can buy a new car every year. At times when we go shopping it is good to ask ourselves, "Do I really need this? Is it my need or my want? Am I buying it out of need or greed?" Actually wanting more than what we really need is stealing from those who are in need.

Consider taking moderate vacations and saving the more extravagant trips for those special occasions, such as anniversaries, family reunions, graduations, etc. Most often, we will remember the people that we spent holidays with more than where we traveled. It really isn't necessary to take lavish vacations every year; simpler vacations can be just as enjoyable. Sometimes we spend too much money traveling afar. We can budget our funds more wisely if we set some money aside to help others survive and also allow funds for our own personal entertainment as well. I can assure you it will be much more satisfying and rewarding than wasting money unnecessarily.

It would be a good idea to go through our closets once in a while to donate to the poor. Learn to share not only what is not used by us, but even goods that can be used by us. Learn to donate things that would be enjoyed and useful to others, instead of items that are worn and no longer of use to us. Realize that what does not belong to us belongs to the poor. Do not get into the practice of hoarding things where they will only be destroyed by time. Learn to give part of your income to charity. It would not be a bad idea to have a *"rice bowl"* for our children not just during Lent, but also throughout the year. They will learn to give from their own sacrifices, and the result of sacrifice is always love.

Occasionally it is good for us to have simple meals. Our meals do not need to be sumptuous and extravagant at all times. It is not the quality of food that creates table fellowship, but the quality of our relationship with each other. We eat to live, not live to eat. Instead of spending extra money on costly diet food items, try reducing your food intake, and the money you save set aside for the poor. How often do we throw away food to clean our refrigerators? Food is precious and a God given gift. Let us teach our children to value and appreciate food. A couple of years ago, I happened to be at a social gathering. At the end of the dinner, one of the children was throwing tantrums and to pacify the child, the mother found a dinner roll, and they were using the roll as a ball, which they were throwing and kicking. What values will the child grow up with? Will not God hold us responsible for what he gives us?

Once in awhile it is a good idea to fast and to experience what millions of our brothers and sisters are living through and feeling everyday. It will make us not only more grateful to God for what we have been blessed with, but we will also become more compassionate to those that are less fortunate, and we will have a desire to help them with their needs.

Relate to the poor with dignity and respect. This again is where the rich man failed in relation to Lazarus. Lazarus was reduced to the level of animals, living in dirt and filth. At times, pet animals have better homes and lives than many human beings. By the grace of God we have been blessed so we should want to share. We never know when our loved ones or when we may need someone's help.

In the eyes of God we are all the same. We are all created in the image and likeness of God. The structure of consciousness in all of us, rich or poor, Asian or American, literate or non-literate is the same. Even if we have nothing to give, at least we can relate to others with respect and dignity. Possessing or having more than others does not make us better human beings. Let us always remember that our own final judgment will be based on how we treated others, especially the poor.

I strongly believe that once we begin to live a spiritual life we will have the desire to be generous and to be compassionate. We will learn to let go and realize that the things we thought would make us happy really cannot. It is only in giving that we receive. It is only when we are empty that God can fill us. Out of this fullness we share and when we share all that we have and all that we are, we become like God.

A priest was talking about the importance of sharing to a group of children attending religion classes. He asked, "Jim, if you had a computer would you give it to Pat?" Jim said, "Of course Father, I would give the computer to Pat." "If you had a baseball bat would you give it to Pat?" asked the priest. Jim said, "Of course, I would give it to my neighbor." "Jim, if you had the latest digital camera, would you give it to Pat?" "Yes, I would give it to Pat," replied Jim. "The beautiful shirt that you are wearing, would you give it to Pat?" "Oh, no Father, I will not give it to Pat," replied Jim. The priest was shocked. He said to Jim, "Jim you were willing to give away the costly goods like your computer, baseball bat, and camera to Pat, but you are not able to give away the shirt that is less expensive?" "Father, I was willing to give away my computer, my baseball bat, and my camera because I do not own those items, but this shirt is the only thing that I have and therefore I cannot give it away."

Share until it hurts to give.

Oh God!

You are a God of justice.

You are a God who harkened to the cry of the poor.

You are a God who made an option for the poor.

You defended the poor against the mighty.

Your Son, Jesus continued your option for the poor.

He said, "Not those who say, 'Lord, Lord' will enter the kingdom of heaven," but only those who see you and serve you in the poor.

Fill me with your grace that your incarnation may continue through me.

Help me to behold you, love you, and to serve you in the poor.

Open my eyes to the situation of the poor.

Let me not be indifferent, but get involved

Let me not be selfish, but learn to share what you have blessed me with

May my life be simple.

When I meet you may I hear the words, "Well done my faithful servant!"

Jealousy: The Destructive Force In Us

And Saul was very angry, and this saying displeased him;
he said, "They have ascribed to David ten thousands,
and to me they have ascribed thousands;
and what more can he have but the kingdom?"
And Saul eyed David from that day on.
—1Samuel 18:8-10

Love is patient and kind; love is not jealous...
—1Cor 13:4

Jealousy: The Undeniable Reality

Once a young couple had gone to see a counselor because the husband was a highly jealous type. The counselor spoke to them for forty-five minutes about jealousy and how if it is not handled properly, it can destroy a good marriage. As they were leaving his office, the counselor could hear the husband reprimanding his wife, "You were looking at him the whole time!" Jealousy!

One evening Adam came home late. Eve was very suspicious so she confronted him. "Adam, you must be seeing another woman." Adam laughed aloud and said to Eve, "Come on Eve, you know that you are the only woman God has created." And the story is, at night, when Adam was fast asleep; Eve was busy counting his ribs. Envy and jealousy!

231

In between news report there was an advertisement about a man who was trying to make holiday reservations in Hawaii. His wife was very excited at the thought of going to Hawaii. In his imagination, her husband visualizes the trainer very close to his wife as he teaches her surfing. Immediately the husband changes his mind and asks his wife, "Honey, how about horseback riding this year?" Insecurity and jealousy!

A pastor shared in his homily, how, after his new associate pastor had celebrated mass on a Sunday morning, most of the people went to wish the new associate well and to congratulate him for his wonderful homily. The pastor was left standing alone, feeling ignored, pangs of jealousy in his heart. Jealousy!

We are with a friend at a casino and he hits the jackpot. Immediately, from nowhere jealously enters our heart. We may smile and say, "I am very happy for you," but deep down inside is there not jealousy in us?

Are we not victims of jealousy when our colleague is promoted in the work place and not us, when our neighbor buys a new car, builds a new house, when someone else is congratulated, when the boss gives attention to someone else and ignores us, when your spouse is deeply engrossed in a conversation with another person? The irony is that we have perfected the art of concealing our true and inner feelings so well that we can give a warm hug to someone and say, "I am so proud of you. You will never know how happy I am for you. You deserve it so much. I am so excited for you," but deep down inside we might be steaming with jealousy. Our hearts, intentions, and actions may not be in harmony. Be honest and ask yourself, "At times, in my life, am I not jealous of others?" What is jealousy and why do we feel jealous?

Before we explore the nature of jealousy, let us admit, that jealousy has been in existence from the time of creation. According to the first book of the Bible, the story of Lucifer and the fallen angels is the story about jealousy; they were jealous of God. In the Garden of Eden, the story of the serpent tempting Eve is a story of jealousy; the devil was jealous of God's intimate relationship with Adam and Eve. Cain was jealous of his brother Abel because God preferred the gifts of Abel to Cain's, and his jealousy drove him to commit murder. The story of the Tower of Babel is the story about humans filled with jealousy and wanting to be like God. Sarah, Abraham's wife, was unable to conceive; she was jealous of Hagar who bore Abraham's child. The brothers of Joseph were jealous of Joseph, who was the favorite of their father. Pharaoh's first born was filled with jealousy against Moses because Pharaoh liked Moses more than his own son. Saul was full of jealousy against David because God preferred David to Saul. The Israelites' enemies were jealous of Yahweh who led the Israelites in victory.

Also, in the New Testament jealousy shows its ugly head among the apostles and the early church. In Luke 9, John complains to Jesus, that someone who did not belong to their group was casting out demons in the name of Jesus. Is not John's complaint motivated by jealousy? Mark 10 presents the story of

James and John asking Jesus to permit them to be seated one at his right and the other at his left. When the other ten hear of this plea they are indignant with James and John. Is not their reaction a manifestation of jealousy? Compared to the other apostles, Paul was more educated and learned. When he became an apostle of Lord Jesus, he was filled with fiery zeal, which got him into trouble in Tarsus. He had to leave Tarsus for Jerusalem. In Jerusalem he was welcomed, but not fully accepted by the apostolic community. Is this not a manifestation of jealousy on the part of the other apostles?

Jealousy has been in existence from the beginning of creation and it will be present until the end of humankind. It is a common experience that all of us, at one time or another, may be jealous of others at various levels and degrees. Jealousy, like the rat that keeps gnawing at the roots of the tree and eventually brings down the tree, has destroyed many individuals and relationships.

What is jealousy really? We could say that it is a feeling, an emotion, an attitude of the mind, sometimes even characterizing the very personality of the person. *Jealous* is defined as "suspicious of a rival or one believed to enjoy an advantage" (The Merriam Webster Dictionary). It is this suspicion that takes the form of a feeling, an emotion or an attitude. Jealousy is like an iceberg whose tip is only seen. Jealousy is an outward manifestation of deep-rooted insecurities and fears of our own lives. The real issue is not jealousy, but lack of courage to face one's own fears and insecurities. For example, the real issue for the husband who was jealous of his wife, who was in the company of her male friends at a social gathering, was not his wife spending time with her male friends, but of his own emotional insecurity. He is not secure and certain of her love for him. There is no room for jealousy if and when he is convinced that her love for him is unique and special and that it can never be compared to love that she has for others. It is his own insecurity that is his problem. Dealing with the tip of the iceberg will not solve the problem, for we are constantly aware that a large chunk of the iceberg is always hidden under the waters. Take the bull by its horns: in all honesty and courage, face the deep-rooted insecurities of life, become aware of them, see through their false nature and drop them.

Saul and David

The real question dealing with jealousy is, "Why do I feel insecure?" In the First Book of Samuel there is a classic passage that addresses this question:

> As they were coming home, when David returned from slaying the Philistine, the women came out of the all the cities of Israel, singing and dancing, to meet King Saul, with timbrels, with songs of joy, and with instruments of music. And the women sang to one another as they made merry,

"Saul has slain his thousands,
and David his ten thousands."
And Saul was very angry, and this saying
displeased him; he said, "They have ascribed
to David ten thousands, and to me they have
ascribed thousands; and what more can he
have but the kingdom?" And Saul eyed David
from that day on. And on the morrow an evil
spirit from God rushed upon Saul, and he
raved within his house, ...(1 Sam 18:6-10).

And the passage continues that Saul was waiting to
kill David. This passage from Samuel shows how
jealousy created anger and anger resulted in a desire
to kill David. Saul's jealousy is only an outward
manifestation of his own fears and insecurities. Saul
was jealous of David, because Saul *compared* himself
to David; he was *not content* with what God had
blessed him with, he *lacked gratitude* to God, and he
had *no true love* for David.

Comparison

One of the deep roots of jealousy is comparison.
Often, don't we compare what we have and ourselves
with others? When Saul heard the women sing, "Saul
has slain his thousands, and David his ten
thousands," he was very angry and resentful. The
women sang the praises of both Saul and David, but
Saul was angry and resentful because he compared
himself and all he had achieved to David. Saul's anger,
resentment and jealousy reveal his own fears and
insecurities. Recently, one of my friends told me
"comparison is the work of the devil." He is absolutely

right. Jealousy comes from comparing what we are and what we have, with others. All the biblical references of jealousy are the result of comparing. The serpent enticed Eve to compare herself with the knowledge of God. Cain compared himself with Abel. The builders of the Tower of Babel compared themselves to God. Pharaoh's first born compared himself to Moses. Joseph's brothers compared themselves to Joseph. Saul compared himself to David, Peter with Paul, the other apostles with James and John.

We are insecure because we keep comparing ourselves: *"I wish I was like her." "I wish I had his talents and gifts." "I wish I had been born in that culture." "I wish I had the looks of that person." "I wish my children were like his children." "I wish my wife was as understanding as his wife." "I wish I had a house like his, like his car, like his job, like his salary..."* and the list goes on. Our wishes never end. Stop comparing yourself and what you have with others. Step out of the "I wish" culture and live in the real world.

Comparisons can be at the physical, cultural, religious, lingual, relational, emotional, and spiritual levels. At the physical level stop comparing yourself with others and realize your gift of uniqueness. Sing and dance with joy because you are a wonder of creation. Jealousy, at the physical level results from the refusal to accept ourselves as God created us and refusing to be happy and contented with that self. When we compare ourselves to others we don't celebrate our own uniqueness. When God created us,

God did not walk down a hall looking at different models in order to create us. The truth is that there has never been another person like you in the entire history of the world and there will never be another person in eternity to come. You are the only one created the way you are in the entire universe. Isn't that something wonderful that needs to be celebrated? God loves variety. God has taken special care to create you and love you just the way you are. Self-acceptance starts with the physical self. This is the way God has created you. Whether I am short or tall, fair or dark or brown, my physical nature is a gift from God. Imagine how uninteresting, boring, and dreary the world would be if everyone looked the same. Thank God, God had better sense and loves variety. Look at nature, the variety among the animals, the fishes, the plants, the flowers, the stars, and the planets. God loves you for what you are and not because of what you may pretend to be.

Do not compare your talents and gifts with those of others. Saul compared his talents with David's. What Saul could not do, David did: killing Goliath. St. Paul reminds us:

> Now there are varieties of gifts, but the same Spirit; and there are varieties of service, but the same Lord; and there are varieties of working, but it is the same God who inspires them all in every one. To each is given the manifestation of the Spirit for the common good. To one is given through the Spirit the utterance of wisdom, and to another the utterance of knowledge according to the same

Spirit, to another faith by the same Spirit, to another gifts of healing by the one Spirit, to another the working of miracles, to another prophecy, to another the ability to distinguish between spirits, to another various kinds of tongues, to another the interpretation of tongues. All these are inspired by one and the same Spirit, who apportions to each one individually as he wills (1 Cor 12:4-11).

St. Paul beautifully says, *"To each is given the manifestation of the Spirit for the common good"* (1 Cor 12:7). The gift is the Spirit itself and the benefit is for the good and growth of the community. Who can claim that he/she does not have the gift of the Spirit? We are all anointed by the Spirit. Each one is called to place his/her gift(s) at the service of the community. The more gifts we have, the more responsibility. It is not the number of gifts that matter, but how we use those gifts for others. All gifts are for the glory of God and for the service of others. The greatest gift that all of us have is the gift to love and to be loved. "So faith, hope, love abide, these three; but the greatest of these is love" (1 Cor 13:13). The secret of life is in living this gift for God and for others. *Stop comparing - start living.*

It is true that no person is absolutely perfect and no person is totally imperfect. There is something good and beautiful about each human being. We have not chosen our birth and all that is associated with the way we are created. We did not ask for it, but it has been given to us. What is given is a gift. A gift is beautiful. In this gift of our own personhood we will find many beautiful and wonderful things that will make us proud. While we delight in our own personhood and all that it implies, we should also rejoice at and be open to other persons, and sincerely appreciate the beauty and goodness that can be found in others, and even enable them to live the beauty and goodness that this person has been given.

Insecurity, and as a result jealousy, can also be present at the level of not accepting oneself emotionally, psychologically, and spiritually as well. Social sciences tell us how different we are from each other. All of us have different personality types. I might be an introvert or an extrovert, a sensate or a thinker. The art of life is to accept myself and stop attempting to be other than what I am. Accepting yourself and working towards balance and integration is what one really needs. Each of us needs to find our own fundamental direction in life, and then try to integrate other directions of life as well. It is not a toss-up between Mary and Martha, but a healthy integration of Mary and Martha in our lives.

Lack of Contentment

Often, we are jealous of others because we are not *contented* with what we have. Saul was not contented with what God had achieved through him. It is true that David killed more Philistines than Saul, but Saul also achieved much as a king. It is this lack of contentment that caused Saul to be jealous of David. We might be blessed with a house, a car, a job, family, children, and material possessions and if we are not contented with what we have, we are planting the first seeds of jealousy in our hearts. It is this lack of contentment that looks at others having more than us, that produces jealousy in us. Craving and desiring more than what we need is closely associated with jealousy. Often in our life when we are jealous of others, let us stop and see whether we are contented with what we have. The more we crave, the more we desire, the more we desire, the more we want, the more we want, the more we crave and the cycle of "wants" never ends. With this cycle we invite suffering unto ourselves. It is only a person with an uncontented heart that is filled with jealousy at what others have. *Learn to be content with what you have.*

Lack of Gratitude

Lack of contentment reveals an *ungrateful heart.* Saul was a non-entity until God chose him, anointed him, and appointed him a King over his people. He ruled Israel for many years. When he turned away from God, God discarded him and chose David. Rather than repenting for his sins and being grateful to God for having chosen him as the first king of Israel, he was jealous of David. Gratitude was missing in Saul's heart. He was not content with what God had given him and where there is no contentment there is no gratitude to God. From the eyes of faith, all that we have is a gift from God's providence. There is no room for jealousy in a heart that praises and thanks God, for every thing that we have is from God. At the end of a sincere, honest, and hard days work whether we have $10 or $100; it is a gift from God. If we are grateful to

God for what God has given us, we will not be jealous of others who have more than us. "Count your blessings." *God dwells in a grateful heart.*

Lack of Love

Saul did not truly love David and that's another reason why he was jealous. In the same passage we read that Jonathan who loved David was not jealous of David. In reality it is Jonathan who should have been jealous of David because Jonathan could not succeed the throne. But Jonathan did not feel jealous, instead he rejoiced with David, because he loved David. Where there is love there will not be jealousy. Love makes you share in the happiness of the other person. Once when I returned to my native country, India, I went to visit the tomb of my father. My brother, who was taking me to the cemetery on his motorcycle, stopped his motorcycle many times and introduced me to his friends saying, "This is my brother who was in Rome." This went on for so many times. He would stop every now and then, and it became embarrassing to me. After sometime I said to my brother, "Enough. You better stop it." He said to me, "In our family none of us has had the chance to go to Rome. You are the only one. I am so happy for you and also proud of you." He was rejoicing with me and sharing my happiness. This was possible because he loves me. He is my brother. In the same way Jonathan loved David, he was not jealous of David. True love rejoices in the good of the other. All that we need to do is to extend that love to others. We need to widen our horizon a little more to include others and love them. When we love others, we will rejoice in the goods of others and cultivate the art of appreciative joy even beyond our own families. Did not Jesus appreciate the faith of the Centurion and praise the gratitude of the Samaritan who returned to give thanks? One who rejoices in the happiness and successes of others will help them to realize their dreams even if they are unable to achieve it in their own life. On the contrary, one who is jealous will not only try to bring down others, but also rejoice in their failures, tragedies, and downfalls.

There were two baskets of crabs, basket *A* containing good-natured crabs and basket *B* containing wicked crabs. At the end of the day when the workers were trying to cover both the baskets the master told them, "It is sufficient to cover only basket *A*, do not take time and effort to cover basket *B*. When the servants asked the master for the rationale behind such a decision, the master replied, "When a crab from the basket *A* tries to climb out of the basket the other crabs will not interfere with the action of the crab. Therefore, we need to cover the basket. But if a crab from the basket *B* tries to escape, all the other crabs will try to pull down the crab that tries to escape. And thus, none of them will be able to leave the basket." The master was right. The following day when the servants returned they found that not a single crab had escaped from basket *B*. At times our human nature is like the crabs in basket *B*. If we are not able to achieve, if we fail or if something is denied to us, out of jealousy we might try to bring down others.

Finally, jealousy is a very strong negative mental reaction. It is vibrant and active especially where the presence of the ego is strong. Human experience tells us that it is not easy to root out negative mental reactions. But nothing is impossible with God's grace. Learn to surrender it to God. In prayer constantly ask God for the grace of a loving heart that will rejoice in the happiness, success, and the good of others. Through prayer and with the help of God's grace we need to work on ourselves. In a deeply spiritual person whose life is constantly animated by the Spirit, there is no room for jealousy. John the Baptist in Mt 3:11 pointing to Jesus says, "... but he who is coming after me is mightier than I, whose sandals I am not worthy to carry; ..." And in Mt 11:11 Jesus talking about John the Baptist says, "Truly, I say to you, among those born of women there has risen no none greater than John the Baptist; ..." John was not jealous of Jesus nor Jesus jealous of John's popularity. When the other apostles are indignant with James and John, Jesus tells them in Mk 10:43-45, "But it shall not be so among you; but whoever would be great among you must be your servant, and whoever would be first among you must be slave of all. For the Son of man also came not to be served but to serve, and to give his life as a ransom for many."

Let us put on the nature of Christ. Christ and jealousy cannot co-exist together. Pray for a loving, compassionate, and an appreciative heart that genuinely rejoices in the well-being and goodness of others.

Jealousy is not part of our true and original nature, for we are created in the image and likeness of God. God is never jealous and God has shared God's nature with us. Because of sin we have lost our original nature, but with God's grace it is possible to chisel away all that prevents our true nature from shining, especially jealousy.

The flowers in the field are not jealous of each other.
Trees growing in each others' shadows in the forest
    are not jealous of each other.
The stars in the blue sky are not jealous of
    one another.
Animals of the forest are not jealous of each other.
It is only we human beings who are jealous of
    each other.

To be jealous is not our true nature.

On a Practical Level

➤ *Remember that by comparison you do more harm to your self than good.*

➤ *Self-love is not a sin. God delights in you for who you are, not what you pretend to be.*

➤ *Count your blessings! In a personal journal or diary record the blessings you receive from God. When you feel jealous of others, go through your personal journal and realize how God has blessed you.*

> Live your life by needs and not by wants.
> Learn the practice of the art of loving-kindness.
> Whenever possible help others to realize their dreams and genuinely share their happiness.
> Pray daily.

Oh God!

I believe that you have created me in your own image and likeness.

Help me to let the spark of your Divine light to shine forth through me.

Through sin I have died to my own original nature.

Let your grace reconnect me to my Christ like nature.

Give me O God, a heart that is free from jealousy and envy.

Recreate in me a pure heart, a heart that rejoices in the happiness, well-being, and successes of others, a heart that is willing to help others to reach their dreams.

Help me to understand that I am unique, may I have the joy of celebrating my uniqueness, my individuality.

Let me not suffer from the evil of comparison.

Make my heart contented and full.

May I rejoice with what I am and what I have.

Bless me with a grateful heart.

Let me never forget that all I have is your gift to me.

Fill me with the Spirit of love, a love that affirms and appreciates others.

Take away my strong ego, may I be humble enough that your mercy may reign in me.

Concluding Words

The pages that you have gone through are an attempt to understand the biblical call to be still and know God. It is a call given to all of us to enter in silence into the depths of our very own being and to be with our God. Doing nothing and just being in the loving presence of God is prayer. Prayer, as an experience of God, not only leads us to an intimate union with God, but it is in this God experience that we realize the true nature of ourselves. It is this realized "self" that is rooted in the indwelling presence of God that permeates our everyday lives. An experience of God in prayer does not take us away from the world, but it enables us to bring God and God's ways into the world that is obsessed with violence, war, terrorism, power, materialism, consumerism, speed, selfishness, jealousy...

It is indeed possible to be the light and salt of the earth!

Pray to be blessed with the gift and the grace of God experience!

In prayer may we realize our true nature.

Through our realized nature may we be blessed with the power to become the change that we wish to see in others and ourselves.